VOLUNTARY ORGANISATIONS

CITIZENSHIP, LEARNING AND CHANGE

ALSO AVAILABLE

ADULT LEARNING IN VOLUNTARY ORGANISATIONS:
CASE STUDIES

VOLUME 1: Case Studies 1 & 2

VOLUME 2: Case Studies 3–13

VOLUME 3: Case Studies 16–30

VOLUME 4: A Town in Action. Voluntary networks in Retford

FROM THE DEPARTMENT OF ADULT EDUCATION, UNIVERSITY OF NOTTINGHAM

Voluntary Organisations
Citizenship, Learning and Change

K.T. Elsdon

with
John Reynolds & Susan Stewart

Published by NIACE, the National Organisation for Adult Learning
and the Department of Adult Education, University of Nottingham

Published by the National Institute of Adult Continuing
Education (England and Wales)
21 De Montfort Street, Leicester LE1 7GE
Company registration no. 2603322
Charity registration no. 1002775
and the Department of Adult Education, University of
Nottingham, Nottingham NG7 2RD

First published 1995

Cataloguing in Publication Data
A CIP record for this title is available from the British
Library

ISBN 1 872941 87 7

Printed & bound by Antony Rowe Ltd, Eastbourne

Contents

Flyout: List of organisations studied, with working titles
Glossary, abbreviations and definitions
Sampling matrix

For
HAROLD MARKS
Public Servant, Adult Educator, Critic and Friend

Acknowledgements

This book attempts to distil six years' research and draw conclusions from it. During so long a period I have been fortunate to accumulate more and deeper debts of gratitude than can be easily enumerated. They are owing first of all to members of the case study groups, of very many other organisations, and the many hundreds of individuals who gave so generously and frankly of their time, often of themselves, and of their hospitality. Our field studies bear public witness to the fascination and delight they shared with us.

The late Professor Michael Stephens, his successors and other Nottingham colleagues have given me a base, generous facilities, and a supportive and friendly working environment. My two colleagues in the research team have been generous so far beyond the call of duty that the project may regard itself as a voluntary organisation in its own right.

Apart from the Nottingham Department's help we have received material assistance from several sources. The Boots Charitable Trust and the Barrow Cadbury Trust have subsidised our publications. During the project's second year its working expenses were met by a grant from the Nuffield Foundation. A Universities Funding Council research grant covered us during years three and four. This met the cost of two half-time appointments and thus built a team with all its benefits for the quality and speed of the work.

When it became known that UFC grants would be limited to two years we faced a crisis. The Barrow Cadbury Trust rescued us. Its Trustees and, especially, its director Eric Baker have contributed far more than the funding that has enabled the project to continue and be completed on schedule: their continuous personal interest in the work and support of the team have been a unique and joyful experience.

The project owes a very great debt to the members of its Advisory Group. Starting with Harold Marks and Richard Mills, it was rapidly joined by Professors Chris Duke and John Field. Professor Keith Percy was also in membership. Mark Dale, who joined later, added more than specialist guidance on computing and statistics to our armoury. The group gave precious time to advice, criticism, suggestions, and personal support. They know that I owe special thanks to Harold Marks, who has been my most relentless though always constructive critic in this and so many previous projects, and to Richard Mills, who added crucial assistance over funding to duties which all members of the group assumed so generously. In addition to them Miss Sheila Browne kindly commented on the final draft in helpful detail. All have contributed; I remain responsible for whatever will be found wanting. My thanks to all.

KTE

Department of Adult Education, University of Nottingham
February 1995

Chapter 1

Introduction

Topic and Purpose

> *Voluntary organisations are important. They make a profoundly effective contribution to the quality of life of the communities in which they operate. It is good for people to belong to societies, and this 'goodness' is passed on from them to others. Having a great many voluntary organisations is a source of justified pride. It is also 'a very British thing'.*

Statements such as this composite but real quotation are articles of faith in our society and some others, a faith which can be supported by a good deal of unsystematic experience. Very little evidence has ever been gathered to confirm, far less to explain them. We do not even know what kinds of voluntary organisations there are, how they are distributed and in what numbers. Nobody seems to have tested the claims to their individual or communal effectiveness. The published literature tends to be historical or generally descriptive, leans towards hagiography and usually deals with the affairs of large national organisations and such lesser or local ones as are mainly concerned with the provision of social services by paid professionals. Both general opinion and the literature – including the most recent and best-known research, e.g. Chanan, 1991 and 1992; Knight, 1993; Volunteer Centre, 1991 – work on this series of assumptions. Some may be incapable of verification. As a result both the public and government remain in the dark. National and local policies, in so far as they exist, rely on vague assumptions, often on prejudice. They may be introduced in the belief that costs will be saved when they are merely transferred. Without better evidence it is, in effect, impossible to argue rationally for or against the practice of shedding statutory responsibilities upon the voluntary sector or even to define what might or might not be good practice there, or to provide suitable advice, support and training to volunteers or professionals and to those who train them. There can be few if any other important aspects of our society of which we are so ignorant without even being aware of it.

It would be foolish to pretend that one research project could bridge such a yawning gap. However, over the last six years the project has addressed the following questions:

- What different kinds of local voluntary organisations are there, and how many? Is it practicable to construct a typology of them?
- What is the formal *and* informal, educational *and* educative impact which voluntary organisations make on individuals, groups and communities?

- How great is it?
- How is it transmitted?
- To whom is it transmitted and how far?

Given answers to such questions:

- What are the origins and characteristics of good practice in different kinds of such organisations, operating in different contexts and with different objectives, and how can such practice be supported and disseminated?
- What are the national and local policy implications?
- What are the implications for training and development?

In pursuing answers we have constructed a typology and carried out 31 case studies across Britain and a locality study (at Retford), in order to gather evidence illustrating the problem area. *(The case study organisations, with their working titles to be used throughout this text, are listed on the flyout at the end of the volume. Brief outline descriptions of their activities are given in Chapter 3. Thirty of the case study organisations and the locality study are published in full: Elsdon, 1991c; Stewart et al., 1992; Elsdon et al., 1993; Reynolds et al., 1994.)*

In this final report we seek to provide such answers to our questions as we have been able to derive from our evidence. They are not invariably exhaustive and may carry varying degrees of conviction, because the evidence itself can sometimes bear shades of interpretation among which we had to choose. There were times when we had to use panga and pickaxe rather than trowel and pruning knife, but we believe we have at least cleared the ground and provided a basis on which more rational policies and action as well as future enquiries can advance with some degree of confidence.

How Many Organisations?

The Centris research (Knight, 1993) placed emphasis on social service-oriented organisations and charities, and arrived at mean incidences ranging from one such organisation to every 204 to 349 individuals of all ages in the population. This project was able to carry out one complete count which indicated an incidence of 1:39.5 in a rural location (Ingleton) and an unpublished survey (private communication) claims 1:50 in a southern commuter village. In the small town of Retford we actually contacted enough to yield a proportion of 1:62, but became aware of additions which produced a likely 1:46. Our research and our general experience do not lead us to suppose that these ratios are other than reasonably representative. If they are projected for the size of the total population of the UK, then they define a range between 1.3 million voluntary organisations, based on Retford, and over 1.5 millions for the accurately known Ingleton total.

These numbers apply to local, membership-based, groups including *autonomous* local branches of more widely based organisations falling within our definition (cf. p. 4). If it were economically practicable to track down not just every church group, every local political party and all their daughter organisations, every cub scout group, first aid or rugby team, these totals would certainly be exceeded substantially. Even our conservative counts and estimates make it safe to assume that there are far more than a million voluntary organisations (VOs) of all kinds in the United Kingdom.

What Kinds of Organisations?

Whatever the accuracy of extrapolations, the total number of VOs in the country is evidently far larger than most people are likely to have realised. We had to begin by trying to disentangle the variety of such bodies contained within this elastic portmanteau. Legally (and without going into the niceties of charity law) it may be assumed to contain everything that is not statutory, and therefore, in today's unlovely jargon, any non-governmental organisation. A cartel of fish-and-chip shops would fit the terminology but could hardly be described as charitable.

Charitable purposes alone would still be an insufficient limitation because they only exclude benefits personal to donors. Eton College is a charity and a VO, but provides benefits specific to its members. So is a charitable trust which dispenses (with or without the help of paid staff and even volunteer workers, as in cases such as the Red Cross) financial aid or benefits in kind. Another type is an organisation (which could be national, regional or even local) which has subscribing members, a governing body of volunteers (usually self-perpetuating rather than elected) which exists to recruit and deploy other, local, volunteers in order to carry out tasks which are determined externally according to the needs of the organisation or service being assisted. Hospital volunteers or the Women's Royal Voluntary Service are instances of this.

These are main types; innumerable intermediate ones occur. What emerges, however, is that they cover the spectrum of well-known and mostly long-established charitable and philanthropic organisations. Among these the best-known tend to be large and to operate from headquarters down to local levels, to have important financial and other resources, and to employ staff who are often numerous. They tend to be governed by more or less self-perpetuating boards which have a strong sense of responsibility to their cause and only a tenuous one to individual members, few of whom may expect to have any influence on policy. These, in turn, do not feel themselves to be part of a functioning democracy. The large agencies, together, are by far the best- or perhaps the only really well-known VOs. For the purposes of our project we have tended to dub them "voluntary agencies" or "volunteer employing agencies" in order to distinguish them from local, self-governing, membership-based organisations.

Our studies provide incontrovertible evidence that these "agencies" are numerically much the smallest segment of the total. They may, like the National Trust or the Automobile Association, have huge numbers of subscribers and call them members although they have neither the rights nor the duties more usually associated with that status. Simple arithmetic based on our own studies, and confirmed by Chanan (1991) and earlier HM Inspectorate of Education surveys, demonstrates the sheer predominance of the *local* autonomous voluntary organisations. These must and do therefore involve and affect a far greater number of people than the very large but few national agencies. In consequence the plethora of small, self-governing, local organisations also has most influence on the quality of life of local communities.

This is not to suggest that big national charitable organisations are anything other than highly influential at their own level and in accordance with their objectives. What is argued here (on the foundation of evidence which will be presented in Chapter 3 and elsewhere) is that, in general, their impact on individual lives and the quality of life in local communities, and on civil society, is less pronounced than that of the very many small local organisations which base their activities on their own membership.

Our Sample Defined

Excepting the Retford locality study, where complete coverage of the voluntary sector was the most important aim, we therefore decided to concentrate our selection of case studies upon local voluntary organisations (LVOs), which we defined as follows:

> For the Project's purposes an LVO is one which draws its membership from a limited area, is based on the principle of personal membership, is self-governing, and pursues objectives which are internal to itself.

This still left within its compass the vast majority of the organisations in all their astonishing variety, ranging from small sports clubs (as within the W London CA) or discussion groups (e.g. the NWR Group) and arts organisations (the Singers) to larger but still local and self-governing umbrella bodies (like Ingleton CA or the Arts Centre). It includes social service organisations with a professional staff if they operate on a genuine membership and volunteer basis (the Settlement), rather than simply as a non-statutory base from which professionals provide services to passive clients. A local Council of Voluntary Services (Bassetlaw) is included, even though it is almost entirely dependent on finance from statutory sources, because it is an independent umbrella body and genuinely democratic under a representative council. The sample also includes an autonomous local group of a national organisation which manages without any finances at all (the NWR Group again). It includes local branches of national and even wider organisations where they are self-governing and run according to their own objectives, such as the National Federation of Women's Institutes, the National Association of Widows and Rotary International; we excluded those which had no such independence. The sample includes the Sutton Volunteer Car Scheme to help us define a borderline between some residual degree of membership and responsibility within an organisation and mere deployment of voluntary labour by an agency.

Local political and religious bodies would have fitted in admirably, but any realistic choice among them would have offended most, and equality of treatment would have played havoc with our sample. We included them in the Retford study with all the more enthusiasm. Several of the churches co-operated generously. The political parties and trade unions ignored us, except for one ladies' luncheon club. We draw no lessons or deductions from this important gap in the response.

The History of the Project

Much research appears, like the North Pole (or, on occasion, the Sahara) simply to exist. Most of what we have read, however, claims valid and respectably altruistic reasons for its origin. We, too, have sought to do so (cf. p. 1f. above). Yet these appear to be relatively superficial motions of the mind, and barely adequate to explain the heady energy that generates research. Whatever tectonic creepings and collisions may have brought a project into existence cannot but influence its theoretical stance, its execution and at least the overtones and undertones of its outcomes. So do subsequent events such as funding, choices of staff and supervision. It therefore seems incumbent upon us to disclose some factors which may have added various tints to our picture.

The project did not, in the first instance, arise from any kind of rational or conventional reflection. The questions we sought to answer (cf. p. 1f. above) presented themselves ready-made to one of us one morning in the shower some 20 years ago, seized his imagination and refused to let go. It seems possible that more creative activities of widely different kinds originate in this manner than it is customary to admit; the dream (so oddly reminiscent of 1 Samuel, 3.) which stimulated the foundation of the Ingleton CA is a dramatic example. Engaged in demanding work and with other commitments, the author of this report sought the co-operation of the Standing Conference on University Teaching and Research in the Education of Adults, which agreed to set up a sub-group to pursue the subject. As the sub-group only recruited one other member (the late Professor H.C. Wiltshire), who was equally busy, it died of inanition and left no trace. Following retirement a number of other projects had priority, and promises had to be kept.

By 1989 the field was clear, and it seemed an attractive prospect to spend about a dozen years carrying out a series of case studies. With hindsight these plans reveal another motive behind the project: simply unorganised curiosity about the infinite variety of "amazing things people get up to", and their reasons for doing so. It was hoped these case studies might subsequently present a younger colleague with the opportunity to draw conclusions and contribute to the understanding of voluntary organisations and their effects. A year passed in preparations and the development of draft typologies and instruments, and 1990–91 was spent on two pilot case studies in order to determine whether the overall plan was practicable and worth while.

Mr Richard Mills and Professor Chris Duke, who had by then joined the project's advisory group, put an end to such lackadaisical proceedings. In the kindliest and most practical manner they suggested that what was in hand was, potentially at least, too urgent to form a gentlemanly agenda for someone's eighth decade. Funding to employ assistance should be sought, the case studies completed, and their import considered not later than March 1995. Having sought advice, it could hardly be ignored. Two colleagues were appointed, who proceeded to insist on treating a half-time engagement as no less full-time than the originator's throughout the vicissitudes (and gaps) of funding. Thanks to their and our main sponsors' generosity, the project has been completed as planned.

The first two case studies were published as volume 1 of our fieldwork in the autumn of 1991, and 13 more as volume 2 a year later. That autumn we submitted our work to date and a tentative interim paper to a seminar which was encouraged to be as critical as possible. We found this even more helpful in the long-run than immediately. The seminar identified the need for a locality study to supplement and cap the individual case studies. It proved practicable to complete these by September 1993 (forming volume 3) five months ahead of schedule, and the uncovenanted period was used to carry out the locality study at Retford (volume 4). After the first two, the case studies were shared equally between team members. A number of papers were written in the course of the project; some of those which were published are listed in the bibliography.

A little more than a year was left in which to analyse and interpret our findings, and write this report. Susan Stewart and John Reynolds have been consulted in the planning and have shared in the critique of the author's drafts. Susan Stewart has prepared some materials for Chapters 2 and 3 and the bibliography, and has compiled the index. In addition to his part in planning and critique of drafts, John Reynolds has carried out the whole of our statistical operations, has guided us in the interpretation of his findings and their qualitative import, and in the process of integrating statistical insights with other field material. His name is not attached to any particular part of this volume but his contribution pervades it.

Methods

Sources and Sampling

The primary sources on which this report rests are 31 case studies (30 of which are published) and the locality study of Retford. Secondary sources are the background literature discussed in Chapter 2, and some other texts. All are listed in the bibliography. What cannot be listed are three different but complementary professional lifetimes of experience, as well as those of our advisory group. Together, they covered the field we were researching and those more formal academic ones which surround it. Here we describe briefly our fieldwork, the methods we used, and the means employed to secure critical supervision and constructive advice throughout the project.

A statistically representative sample of the universe of British LVOs would have had to be impracticably large and complex. The solution adopted to overcome the problem was John Reynolds' matrix (reprinted on the reverse of the flyout). This consists of a grid which distinguishes seven main groups of organisational objectives of LVOs on its horizontal axis and seven main groups of personal objectives of LVO members on the vertical. Seven important subordinate characteristics of LVOs were identified for each of the 49 boxes of the grid, yielding altogether 343 potential descriptors.

Having constructed this framework for a typology, we then had to select individual LVOs which, between them, covered the field. Since all fulfilled the conditions of several descriptors, the range was covered with a total of 29. Two were duplicated, yielding a total of 31 case studies. In selecting organisations to be studied we were able to rely upon the knowledge of the field which was represented by the research team and the advisory group, or accessible to them.

The first and invariable criterion for selection was the need accurately to fill specific gaps in the grid, in order to secure a total grouping which would be credibly representative of the field in Scotland, England and Wales. A study of the matrix (cf. flyout) will confirm this. However, in many instances this left a choice, where we employed different criteria. One of our objectives was to create a kind of thesaurus of good practice. Therefore, other things being equal, we preferred organisations which were judged (by the criteria of their own aims) to be successful, although others were not excluded and contributed valuable insights. If there was further scope for choice without introducing bias we tried to choose more rather than less economically accessible locations. Finally, and with care not to distort overall balance, we allowed for a minor concentration in North and West Nottinghamshire, in order to deepen our understanding of the interaction of LVOs with each other and the community at large. It also saved scarce funds.

However, studies of organisations in isolation were failing to lead us to a full understanding of their impact. To address this, the seminar referred to earlier suggested that the case studies should be complemented by locality studies, i.e. attempts to try and track down all the VOs in particular localities, to find out their main characteristics, and to study their interaction with each other and with the public services, business and industry, and the professions. As the introduction to volume 4 of our field studies (Reynolds *et al.*, 1994, p. 1f) explains, this is a vast task even in a small town. Within our resources it could only be attempted once, but we would argue that *for the present purpose*, once is enough, since the *principles and mechanics* of these network interactions and their effects were substantially revealed by the exercise. They are likely to be the same elsewhere, though different conditions and policies would produce other practical outcomes from them.

Execution

It remains to explain how the case studies were executed. Case studies 3 and 31 were undertaken jointly by the whole teamwhen the two colleagues first joined it, in order to establish common methods and standards of interviewing, observation and recording. They were then written up individually. All other case studies were undertaken individually, but to a common pattern and with the help of a common aide-memoire for the interviews. This reflects the fundamental question-areas which underlie the project as a whole (cf. p. 1f. above and Appendix 1 for the aide-memoire).

Each case study rests upon study and observation of the organisation, its context and relevant aspects of its history, and especially on a programme of interviews with members individually or in small groups. There were interviews with members of staff where any were employed, and always with outside individuals who had knowledge of the organisations and their members, and could furnish independent evidence.

Interviews were conducted on the basis of an aide-memoire as opposed to questionnaires. This helped to encourage respondents to talk freely to us and avoided biasing or limiting their response with set questions. Moreover, the aide-memoire provided a common framework within which what each respondent said could be recorded in a manner which made all the 831 individual records immediately comparable. The same framework was used subsequently in writing up each case study, and strongly affects the pattern of this volume.

It was important to avoid placing reliance solely upon members of the organisations for our evidence. However critical or observant (or excessively modest) some of these might be, their testimony in total represents just one dimension of evidence. Where staff were employed, all or, in very few instances, most were interviewed, and added a further dimension, if not an entirely independent one. The crucial third dimension was provided by a third group, whom we dubbed observers. Some, such as officers and elected members of local authorities, had official contact with the LVOs concerned. Others – e.g. journalists, social workers, librarians or clergy – had observation of local groups and their activities and performance as part of their role. Some people simply knew an organisation and its effects through contact with its members and activities, without being personally involved. The essence of the method was twofold: the multi-dimensional approach secured the highest practicable degree of realism and reliability, and it enabled us to use the different groups of respondents as cross-checks upon each other.

There is no statistical significance in the number of interviews obtained from, or about, each organisation. High proportions of respondents to membership were usually achieved in small and medium-sized groups and lower ones in the big organisations. On the other hand, the last, being better known, yielded more observer comment.

The choice of respondents from among the members varied since we were very much in the LVOs' hands. With some, especially small groups, it was possible to gather volunteers from a full meeting. Mostly the secretary or others helped by setting up interviews in the first instance. All

the organisations were as helpful as they knew how; the differences between selection arrangements seemed to reflect size, and the tightness of
organisation. In each instance we tried to interview as representative a
spread of members as possible. A few groups (or their secretaries) per-
sisted in believing that committee and other "expert" members would
make more helpful respondents. Such imbalances, whether due to
chance or misguided helpfulness, became noticeable almost at once, and
we took steps to correct them. In addition, as noted above, we obtained
interviews wherever possible with knowledgeable outside observers.
Only in UIMWO did we gain an impression of being largely confined to
paid staff.

In most instances the interview programme was supplemented by a
penumbra of informal conversations with a variety of people who added
pieces to the jigsaw. There were at least 150 but probably as many as 250
of these. Note was taken of them, but they were not recorded in detail
like the main group of 831 full and formal interviews. This total consists
of 552 members of the organisations, 68 paid members of staff, and 211
of those we designate "observers".

There was thus a substantial total of independent evidence but it
must be admitted that secondary evidence of the effects of membership
on individuals proved more difficult to obtain than any other. This particular link in the chain of transmission is therefore less strongly represented in our evidence than any other. The existence and real strength of
the link could, in many instances, be inferred by projection from testimony obtained as it were on either side of it. We admit, however, that in-
ference is less powerful than direct evidence.

We chose to record the interviews manually. Tape recording limits
especially the least articulate and socially competent, and preserves
everything, however irrelevant. In consequence it is enormously costly in
clerical and professional time. It is, of course, relatively more reliable,
simply because of its totality. We wanted to secure an equal degree of reliability, but together with maximum relevance, and in addition as much
useful verbatim quotation as possible. To secure this we needed interviewers who were thoroughly experienced, practised observers who
knew the field well enough to distinguish what was relevant and to
avoid bias. As note takers they had to be skilled, accurate and tactful.
They also had to be acceptable to a wide variety of people, and know
how to prompt respondents when necessary, but not lead them. Finally,
they had to be able to write up records accurately, and prepare their case
studies for publication. Owing to the way in which the limited funds
were deployed we had a team with the necessary experience.

The interview programme could not be relied upon to obtain full
personal and employment details and the history of each respondent's
participation in the whole range of formal and informal, voluntary and
statutory educational and leisure activities, both prior to joining the LVO
being studied and currently, or to relate levels and kinds of participation
to all personal details including terminal education age (TEA). We therefore used individual anonymous questionnaires (reproduced in Appendix 2) in 10 LVOs where this practice promised to be most productive. A

total of 157 such returns were obtained. They proved valuable both to the study of particular organisations and in generalised form.

The Case Studies

Conducting the enquiries for each case study in the manner we describe – i.e. by as it were putting each respondent and each organisation in the lead, with ourselves prompting where necessary and recording – made each of them a literally extraordinary experience. Virtually everywhere and by everyone we were overwhelmed by helpfulness, hospitality and an eager enthusiasm. Respondents blended interest in what we were do- ing and a desire to assist us with great generosity in sharing with us not just their interests but, often, intimate feelings about these and their lives. We had expected to learn much about LVOs and their members, but the quality, the intensity and the intimacy of what was so freely given to us remain unforgettable.

People were almost always deeply modest about what they were do- ing and usually underestimated its interest and importance. It was, we believe, the fact that (rather than facing them with a set of closed ques- tions) we were really listening to them, valuing what they told us, and actually writing it down in preparation for a publication, that caused them to react as they did. The outcome was not just our learning; people told us again and again they felt that in responding to us they were dis- covering themselves and their activities and their organisations, seeing all this in a new light, newly aware of the springs of some of their actions and of their own worth. It is not surprising that many organisations told us they had learned much from being studied and that this learning con- tributed to their confidence and their development. What the research team learned will be evident from our texts.

What we report of these relationships will rightly raise the question how far they may have added to the normal tendency of respondents to give answers which they assume will please and help their interlocutors. The fact that a high proportion of the case study organisations were good examples of their kind increased the risk of such collusion. We can only answer that we have been well aware of it, that team members watched over each other to counteract tendencies to "go native", and that the ad- visory group challenged us whenever it seemed appropriate.

The standard procedure for writing up case studies for publication involved producing a draft from all the interview records and other ob- servations and the anonymous questionnaires where these were avail- able. This was circulated first to the team, amended or re-written, and then to the advisory group for their criticism and suggestions. A copy also went in confidence to the appropriate representative of the LVO concerned, with the request to note any factual inaccuracies, or state- ments whose publication could embarrass either individuals or the or- ganisation. It was made clear that the findings as such were not for discussion, but LVOs were given the option of anonymity. Surprisingly this was accepted only twice, though in two other instances we insisted on using a pseudonym to protect individuals.

The Locality Study

For the locality study of Retford a different approach had to be used. The limited time available did not permit piloting and we were fortunate that the method we adopted proved reasonably effective. It involved the initial use of postal questionnaires (cf. Appendix 3). A very high proportion of these were followed up with interviews, both face to face and by telephone. Many interviews then led to contact with organisations not originally known to us. Details sufficient for processing were thus obtained either by questionnaire returns or by interview, or both, of 101 organisations. Two hundred and thirty-four others were definitely identified, making a total of 335 known to exist. Collection of further information produced a likely minimum total of 450. In addition to the 101 usable responses from voluntary organisations there were 15 interviews with "observers" – including non-members, representatives of the other organisational targets and of the public services. A large number of additional contacts were not formally recorded. Full details appear in Reynolds *et al.* (1994).

The Final Report

For this final report all the sources which have been outlined were available. They were used in their verbal form, but also explored statistically. Two data bases were created in addition to the existing Retford one: the first took account of every one of the 831 individuals who had been interviewed, and the second, much smaller and simpler one, rests on the 157 anonymous questionnaires returned by members of the 10 case study organisations for which they were used. The degree to which questionnaire returns are or are not representative of the whole memberships concerned is known by comparing them with the interview responses and with whatever overall information was available from the groups. Any differences were taken into account when the questionnaires were interpreted for the case studies. When *generally* compared with the large data base, they are probably somewhat unrepresentative because they reflect a population which is rather more ready to put pen to paper. This is inherent in the choice of organisations included in the smaller sample.

To sum up, the information sources for both the 31 individual case studies and this final report were as follows:

Case study individual interview records	
(including 552 members, 68 paid staff and 211 observers)	831
Case study individual questionnaires	157
Retford individual returns/interviews	101
Retford observer interviews	15
Case studies	31

There was thus a sum-total of 1,104 formally recorded interview and questionnaire responses and up to some 250 additional informal case study observer interviews. Appendix 5 describes the statistical procedures which have been used, gives details of the three data bases, and lists other archive materials which are held.

The main data base was created by translating, as far as practicable, the interview with each individual into categories and, where possible, quantifying these. This yielded a potential 107 separate descriptive items for each individual who had been interviewed. Allowance was made for instances in which "no information" was the appropriate entry for any category.

One hundred and seven variables proved necessary to reflect all the information which had been collected about the organisations, the individuals, the variety of learning and change, and the ripples of transmission from individuals and groups out into the community. Characteristics such as age, sex, TEA, and also properties such as committee membership or other responsibilities are factual and easily recognised. Categorising members' objectives was also generally straightforward, and so was the distinction between these and outcomes.

On the other hand variables such as "has increased respondent's range of social contacts", "improved ability to co-operate", "skills are transmitted", or "leads to more independent living" differ from factual data such as age. The degree to which they occur in an individual cannot be stated because of the variations between different respondents and their "starting points", and also the ways in which they perceived the changes which they claimed had taken place in themselves. Where strict comparisons were impracticable, quantification could not be attempted.

Nevertheless the changes of which people spoke, often with feeling and practical illustrations, or corroboration by observers, could be categorised without quantification, and entered simply under yes, no, or no information. The very large number of entries which resulted was recorded in order to reflect the wide variety of learning and change which respondents reported to us. It proved practicable, subsequently, to group some of the closely related ones for statistical analysis, but only a faithfully complete initial record could make that analysis and any eventual synthesis credible.

We do not claim that the changes which people reported under the many variables occurred solely as a result of their membership of LVOs. What we are able to assert is that all the information gathered and represented in the variables and the data base came from the respondents, and from them only. Many spoke with conviction and feeling of the often substantial extent to which they had changed in relation to particular variables. The interview records include a very large number of specific illustrations of altered outlook, increased knowledge, skills and confidence, and ability to control one's own life.

The important finding is that these developments have taken place, and that people perceived them as permanent changes in themselves, which they very often attributed to their membership of an LVO. Variation in the degree of change in the variables does not invalidate the comparisons made by the respondents themselves, or any generalisations which emerge from these. Moreover, the effects were often confirmed by external and independent evidence. Finally, where there is evidence of benefits to the communities concerned, this reflects confirmation back on to the individuals within organisations who are responsible for them.

Supervision, and Some Theoretical Issues

From the start of the project our practice had to prove the case for our chosen method of recording interviews. More important, we felt that the project should, throughout its life, be subject to the most stringent as well as constructive criticism available. To secure this, rather than set up a steering committee to meet at regular intervals, we created an advisory group of, eventually, six members. Together they represented what we considered to be the best available expertise in relation to different aspects of the project. They were prepared to devote time and thought to the critique of any plans and working papers, and to each of our drafts as it emerged. The advisory group therefore worked intensively by post, occasionally by telephone, and only rarely (when there were issues that needed group discussion) face to face. The process proved more useful – and, incidentally, more economical – than a conventional research steering committee. It did, however, make great demands upon group members, and time saved from travel was deployed into activity which benefited the project.

The issue of objectivity may be considered in this context. It would be ridiculous to pretend that a team of individuals who had themselves been much involved in the field could be unmoved by the project or by what they found in the course of their field work. Subsidiary aims such as the hoped for creation of "a thesaurus of good practice" are evidence of this, and so is the implication of a system of values which inheres in the assumption that some practices are *good* – which would mean that others are therefore bad or at least less desirable.

We gladly admit that a degree of subjectivity is implied in the system of values and consequent judgments which underlie the whole of this research project and which are most fully expressed in our final chapters. We deny that this kind of subjectivity invalidates our findings. Indeed, we would argue that objectivity in any transaction between human beings (whether direct or through the medium of a questionnaire) is literally a non-sense: objectivity between subjects is a will-o'-the-wisp. What can be realistically and usefully aimed for is something quite different, namely a subjectivity which is sensitive, accurately informed, both conscious and conscientious, and which holds a responsible balance between valuing and evaluating what it observes. This has been our aim. Our advisory group has kept watchful eyes upon our pursuit of it. We must leave it to readers of our field evidence and this volume to decide if we have kept it in sight.

We have been criticised from the very start of the project for two serious omissions. Both are deliberate. We have refused to set up hypotheses to prove or disprove, or to locate the project within any form of social theory. Hypotheses have a way of being self-fulfilling, and theories of creating their own universe. But we have been researching relatively new territory, and our aim has been to understand and to map it in its own right. We wanted people and organisations to speak for themselves and from their own experience, not to fit them into some neat academic bed of Procrustes. Had we done so we should have risked corrupting our findings.

In this we have followed a well-established if currently less fashionable path of social and educational research with analogous aims (e.g. Harris and Molloy, ND; Spencer, 1964; Mee and Wiltshire, 1978). Moreover, during the five years of fieldwork we abstained from indulgence in generalisations and conclusions, however hedged about with modesty and tentativeness. Now that fieldwork is completed, our observations (albeit subjective in the sense we have admitted) permit us to draw certain conclusions and offer some generalisations. These, in turn, allow hypotheses to be erected. The knowledge we have produced may be used to varying degrees in support of several social theories. We leave it to the proponents of these approaches to do so.

However, before we proceed to give some account of our findings and what they signify, it is necessary to set them in their context by discussing what was done, thought and written in our field before we started and up to very recently (Chapter 2). Chapter 3 continues to establish the background to our work by means of brief outline descriptions of the sample organisations and relates them to a very general model of the composition, size and general shape of the universe of local voluntary organisations and some characteristics of their members. Chapter 4 presents, in general terms, our findings about the known objectives of organisations and their outcomes as reported by their members, and seeks to discover the significance of parallels and incongruences between them. This is followed by four central chapters (5, 6, 7 and 8) devoted to accounts of learning and change in individuals, in organisations and in local communities. From these we move outwards again, first to the relationship between some processes touched upon in preceding chapters, and their outcomes at all levels (Chapter 9). This includes findings about the nature and effects of special factors such as leadership and relationships between members and staff, lay and professional, in LVOs, and about particularly significant general outcomes such as "active citizenship". Chapter 10 summarises the practical and policy implications of our findings at all levels from the individual organisation to central government. Appendix 6 closes the circle by considering some remaining gaps in our knowledge and new ones which have been opened by our enquiry.

A minor textual point must be made here. A book such as this lacks space for the numerous verbatim quotations from our respondents which were part of the fabric of our fieldwork volumes. Single quotation marks denote verbatim evidence where it occurs in the present text.

Chapter 2

Some Contexts for the Enquiry

To consider the whole history and literature of VOs in Britain could fill several volumes. To treat them separately here would demand more space than seems justified. This chapter attempts to combine them by focusing briefly and eclectically on what seems to illuminate our topic, and setting it against this developing background, down to some current trends.

The vague assumptions mentioned at the start of the preceding chapter are widely held. The likeliest reason is that most of the VOs which come readily to people's minds are the philanthropic agencies which serve charitable and worthy ends: "good causes" from Oxfam, the St John Ambulance Brigade or the Salvation Army to old people's luncheon clubs and charity shops. Further thought may bring the National Federation of Women's Institutes, the Workers' Educational Association or the British Legion to mind, but few members of the public will associate a local allotment society, church choir, darts club or self-help group, whatever its purpose, with talk of voluntary organisations. What is so personal, usually small and modest, and almost always very informal, hardly seems to deserve the dignity of formal terminology. It does not seem to belong to the same category as the activities of people who have London headquarters and leap into action to tackle catastrophe at the ends of the earth.

Popular misunderstanding of the organisational and numerical distribution of VOs is reinforced by the literature of the subject. Studies of major philanthropic agencies abound. Even those, less common ones, which are, like Aspinall (1988) or Jerman (1981), within our definition of LVOs for the purposes of the project, tend to concentrate on history, structure, events and, perhaps, methods. Only rare exceptions pay attention either to social and economic contexts at one extreme or to effects at the other. One of these is the account by Clarke (1990) and his co-authors of the history, principles and practice of the community centres movement together with its educational, social and economic contexts. This chapter owes a substantial debt to its pioneering research and its text. Social structures and social change tend to preoccupy action research and social surveys even where these are intensive and localised, like Spencer (1964) and Stacey (1960 and 1975). The same limitations apply to major national reports, which will be discussed shortly.

The only recent large scale attempt to gather statistics of volunteering, the Volunteer Centre's 1991 *National Survey of Voluntary Activity*, provides impressive totals as well as evidence of overall growth. It shows for the first time that new volunteers tend to gravitate more towards environmental and developmental activities than conventional philanthropy, while some major old-established agencies complain of a shortage. There is also important information about the social class, age and sex distribution of the body of volunteers. These latter findings compare closely with our own (cf. Chapter 3 below).

The survey's extrapolations suggest a total minimum involvement of as many as 51% of adults, or 23 millions, in the UK. However, most of these (68%) had been involved in money raising, and the statistics of time spent in volunteering suggest that much of this is low level activity with collecting tins and distribution of envelopes rather than participation as a full member in an organisation. This particular detail, together with some others, creates a significant impression that these statistics are heavily biased towards volunteering in support of agencies and the philanthropic sector. Apart from sports and exercise there is mention only of religious, environmental, political and human rights groups. It seems possible that here, as in other general works on the voluntary sector, the bulk of autonomous local activity escaped notice, or the term "voluntary organisation" is defined so as to exclude it.

The Influence of Government

Political developments such as Care in the Community legislation and its administrative consequences appear to have been the main inspiration of important recent studies such as Chanan's (1991 and 1992), Knight's (1993) and a large-scale international study at present in progress (Knapp and Kendall, 1991). A questionnaire distributed by the European Community appeared to be addressing the same area of activity. Except for Chanan, and, to some extent, Knight, they seem to assume that most VOs are large, hierarchical, paternalistic, and professionally staffed, although they may also employ volunteers. Furthermore, it is assumed that their purpose lies largely in the area of caring, relief, welfare and social development, *and that this purpose can be used or adapted to take over tasks previously performed by the public sector.* These are organisations which exist for the sake of services to be provided for clients, and not to meet the needs or objectives of any volunteers employed by them, even where these are termed "members". It is therefore their structure, organisation and finance which are of predominant interest to researchers, rather than their impact on the volunteers.

This concentration on structural and social welfare issues is of particular importance in the current British context of "contracting out" public services to voluntary organisations. The effects of this policy on the structure, finance and activities of these organisations, and the consequential effects upon neighbourhoods and individual members, are often fundamental. This gives special importance to Knight's (1993) findings and his critique of the "contract culture". His consequential proposals for major changes in the definition of charitable status cannot be ignored, regardless of whether they win support. It may be a moot point whether he would have made them in this form if his statistics had given him access to a more complete and balanced picture of the voluntary field. We shall return to these matters in the context of our own field evidence and in Chapters 7 and 9. The phenomenon of the contract culture and its malign consequences are by no means confined to the UK, as noted in Chanan's (1992) European studies and a context as different as India, where many VOs have become almost instruments of government (Tandon, 1994).

LVOs and their Literature

Some of these issues and most of the major reports have at any rate some relevance to the much larger field of mainly local organisations which serve the interests and concerns of their members and are democratically controlled by them. Having decided to investigate this largely unexplored field, we had to look for a context for it and for its literature. Because the general run of LVOs, and especially their individual and social effects, had not been studied we had to search a rather wider range of literature for sources of illumination. There was descriptive material, including sometimes obvious accounts of what volunteers *do*. No evaluative information other than HM Inspectorate of Education papers and reports was discovered. However, what we were looking for in particular was evidence of thinking about learning and change in the context of leisure interests and concerns, about self-government and democratic responsibility, and about their relationship to local communities and their quality of life. This turned out to be sparse, and scattered over a wide range of sometimes tenuous connections.

Organisations serving cultural and intellectual leisure are naturally more vocal and more literate than others. Thus the history and the constitutions of early literary and philosophical societies, such as were founded in most county towns and survive not uncommonly, are better known than those of football clubs and allotment societies. The Corresponding Societies and Adult Schools have their own literature. The working men's colleges (despite the Revd Vaughan's "Sirs, ye are brethren" above the door) were more institutional than democratic, but a number especially of early WEA branches have attracted their own historians (e.g. Allaway and Rawson, 1954). However, as far as we have been able to establish, none of these studies seems to have concerned itself in any substantial degree with the personal effects on members or the broader ones on local communities. Their intentions were no less valid than ours, but different. Moreover, it might well be hazardous to undertake our task in any but a contemporary context, when living witnesses can give their evidence.

Settlements and Community Associations

Of greater importance for our own task have been works devoted to the development of settlements, adult education centres, community associations and centres. There are also some references to the voluntary sector generally in major studies and reports which are only tangentially connected with our topic. The settlements have much to contribute. A minority among them presents some structural differences from the mainstream. These were significant in themselves and also point forward to some problems which were later reflected in the community association and adult education centre movements. These contrasts help towards an understanding of current tendencies in the relationship between professional staff and lay memberships, which will be more fully discussed in Chapter 9.

Most settlements, with their powerful groups of young university men in residence, were in a good position to develop rather more egalitarian approaches than might have been expected in late Victorian philanthropic institutions. Thus Briggs and Macartney (1984) and Pimlott (1935) found a convincing basis of individual membership at Toynbee Hall from 1885. They report that self-governing clubs were the most significant activity in "the majority of settlements" as early as 1935.

The contrast with the minority is significant. One women's settlement for instance, founded by the philanthropic wives of a group of businessmen, employed an unmarried lady social worker to carry out apparently limitless welfare work on their behalf and under their control until she could cope no longer and had to be replaced by another. It may be typical of conditions around the turn of the century that she remained grateful, and happy with the arrangements.

The structure and attitudes here were not untypical of such VOs or rather agencies, more often than not founded by members of evangelical religious organisations, which kept *professional* control in the hands of a self-perpetuating lay group and employed professionals on tasks most of which might more appropriately have been undertaken by committee members or other volunteers from among a membership which, if it existed, had no significant rights or duties. The professionals were not uncommonly employed under exceptionally poor conditions and terms possibly modelled on lady committee members' domestic arrangements. It seems to have been expected that they would wish to make personal sacrifices for the sake of the privilege of serving a good cause. As an alternative such posts, as well as, later, some centre wardenships were sometimes filled by members (not invariably well-qualified) of the sponsoring group whose private incomes enabled them to waive emoluments.

Space had to be devoted to a minority of problem organisations because the structures and attitudes they bred are not extinct. They may well have contributed to the failure of democratic control and member responsibility to develop more actively in what we term "agencies" – i.e. the well-known, old-established philanthropic organisations – and why some of these are to-day short of volunteers while others face no such problem (Knight, 1993). Moreover, the same attitudes were quickly transferred to some of the voluntary adult education centres which were founded in the years just before and after the First World War, attitudes which hindered development in that minority group.

Once again a series of initiatives from religious groups were responsible for the foundation and early development of these centres. Ideas drawn from the Adult Schools, the Settlements, the University Extension movement and the Danish Folk High Schools were combined with the

Quaker tradition of an inclusive and strongly democratic self-governing membership to create a number of what were intended to be non-residential settlements, or community centres with a specific but broadly conceived adult education remit. The case was first fully stated in British Institute of Adult Education (1924). Allaway (1977) outlines the history to that date and Elsdon (1962) discusses the centres, their structure and practice. Both the programmes of the early centres and their practice in recruiting young graduate volunteers to teach classes and form self-governing clubs are reminiscent of Toynbee Hall and the working men's colleges.

However, a few of the centres were caught in the structural and attitudinal trap that has been described. These took longer than others to adopt appropriate constitutional patterns and sensible ways of deploying paid professional staff before they developed their full potential. But the conception of self-governing, membership-based adult education centres was powerful. Ideally, they saw themselves as "a hearth and home for adult education". They offered a wide range of subjects for study at a variety of levels as well as a variety of informal leisure activities, and they had a concern for service to the local community and beyond. The idea and its practice caught the imagination of a wide variety of opinion leaders during the rapid development of LEA adult education from the 1950s on and resulted in successful groups of autonomous LEA centres, e.g. in Kent (Jessup, 1951), Cumberland, South Wales and elsewhere. Nottingham University was a notable contributor, with a string of similar centres. Few of the entirely voluntary centres survived unchanged, or at all, the funding crises and fee inflation of the last 20 years. Yet with recent additional destructive changes it may become the duty of the voluntary centre to save what little remains from the wreck of LEA general adult education.

The next major and more widespread development of significance to our work is the community association and centre movement which is so well described in Clarke (1990). Its authors demonstrate its origin as being linked especially to the development of huge new housing estates, mostly without communal facilities, after the First World War. They see the associations, and their centres as these became available, as initially analogous to councils of social service, but at a more local level. They also relate them to the adult education centres because of the way they linked voluntary and statutory services, formal and informal educational and leisure pursuits with each other under autonomous democratic control, though usually in reverse proportion. More than these, however, they developed a capacity for linking *all* other local organisations with themselves and thus becoming genuine representatives of their neighbourhood.

The perception that informal learning "goes on whether we know it or want it or not", the practice of formal provision informally delivered, education for "democratic organisation and social responsibility" in running, for instance, a table tennis club, and the duty to disperse all kinds of responsibilities as widely as possible – all these and much more are found in principle and in the earthiest of practice in Marks (1949), a thoroughly up-to-date pamphlet which was, surprisingly, never reprinted. The same emphasis on community associations *and* adult education centres, as informal but dynamic educative forces for the community and for their individual members, radiated from the extraordinarily influential contribution of Frank Milligan. It was made almost exclusively through the spoken word and personal example, but some idea of its quality emerges from Groombridge (1976).

Given success in this community-wide role (of which our own study of Ingleton CA is an outstanding example), the internal linking and external representation demand and foster a skilled dedication to local democracy in a manner which was new. Our case studies (especially Ingleton CA, Guildhouse, the Arts Centre, the WI Group, Bassetlaw CVS, the Settlement, the Residents' Association, and Mountain Rescue) demonstrate it consistently as a major though not necessarily a premeditated function of local voluntary organisations (Harris and Molloy, ND).

New Stimuli

The community association movement and other activities in the area of sport and youth and community work, and the idea and practice of voluntary control in autonomous organisations, received a further impetus from the Physical Training and Recreation Act of 1937. Its main purpose was, no doubt, to prepare a fitter nation for approaching war. Its effect was to establish in the minds of Local Authorities and other funding bodies the importance of democratic, self-governing VOs and their need for a physical base. It also defined the possibility of co-operation and financial partnership between LVOs, their members and statutory bodies.

The general ferment of ideas created by the 1939–45 war and preparations for peace added immeasurably. The work of army education and the Army Bureau of Current Affairs had been hugely influential, and so were local neighbourhood groups. Both encouraged and developed democratic practice and democratic skills at most levels, and among the educationally least privileged in particular. The Council for Education in Music and the Arts (CEMA, which became the Arts Council) and much later the Sports Council were able to build their encouragement of local autonomous activity on these foundations.

The idea that a local community's quality of life would be permanently enhanced by public help in setting up and feeding (but not taking over) a wide variety of autonomous cultural, sporting and leisure activities came to be widely accepted, even if it was to take many years for more than a tiny number of LAs to act upon it. Recent legislative and other changes introduced by government have reversed financial policies in this regard. However, they have not yet been widely successful in making the public or LAs alter their concepts of civic duty or the public its expectations. The multiplicity of local societies which owe their origin to the original stimuli shows no signs of wilting.

The famous "Red Book" on *Community Centres*, the new Ministry of Education's first publication (1944), gave specific support to the principle underlying the community association movement, that people could learn to create and run their own representative organisations. They would use them to improve their neighbourhood's quality of life if voluntary and statutory resources were meshed with each other. It was published in 1944 and reprinted twice – but significantly not after 1950, by which time governments were losing faith in too much autonomy and what they conceived to be its costs.

The same principle was being applied in the post-war years by British colonial civil servants in West Africa and sparked off the community development movement. The term itself has been too widely applied to a variety of other, sometimes covertly authoritarian approaches. The practice, however, remains perhaps the most powerful instrument of social, economic and civic change in a community: it combines individual and social learning and change, seconded but never replaced, by professional skill and public resources. Its importance was quickly perceived by the British Council, whose "kit", including Batten's handbook, triggered much development in the USA in particular. Most home-based professionals lagged behind and in the UK the movement's influence came to be felt through a few individuals and later through Batten's teaching and publications (Batten, 1957, 1965, 1967).

The development of New Towns and overspill and other public housing estates stimulated research which sometimes throws light on our concerns. It included Spencer's (1964) finding that mobile majorities (those who could afford either a car or the cost of other transport) had developed, whose members had stronger links to interest and work-based than to geographical communities. The non-mobile, on the other hand (often married women, the old and the young and generally poorer people), tended, perhaps perforce, to prefer more local activities. Because these had to find a widely acceptable common denominator they tended to be sociable and mainly passive. Whether it was cause, outcome or both, the result, as Clarke (1990) and others note, was a rapid specialisation on interest or group lines. This expressed itself in the growth of organisations such as the Women's Institutes, Townswomen's Guilds, and the National Housewives' (later Women's) Register, of new specialist organisations and clubs (our Archaeologists, Singers and Railway Trust are obvious examples) and the accelerated growth of enrolments in general adult education.

Following the seminal research of Joseph Trenaman, originally published in 1957, all this was indeed predicted as an outcome of the raising of the school leaving age in 1947 and the concurrent rapid growth of grammar school education. The improvements of the 1919 Education Act, reinforced by wartime Forces education, had caused the earlier post-war boom in enrolments. In the same way, by the 1960s another new generation of better educated and less deferential adults had reached the age when their initial familial and career preoccupations would recede, and leave them ready to participate in active cultural and other leisure pursuits.

There was thus a rapidly expanding new public of individuals who were eager to involve themselves actively and responsibly in a variety of pursuits and developmental activities, and consequently an extremely

rapid growth of these. From the late 1960s central government inter-
vened through a variety of new schemes which stimulated or required
local voluntary participation. They included Urban Aid, the Home Office
Community Development Project, and the joint Departments of the Environment and Education experiment on *Leisure and the Quality of Life*
(1977). The rapid growth of Arts Council and Sports Council activity
aided provision of local arts and sports centres. The latter, especially,
were not uncommonly the result of statutory and voluntary co-operation.

Few of these developments saw voluntary involvement much beyond the formation of committees to apply for and administer funds, although these included some members of the public as well as councillors
and officials. Responsible membership or volunteer leadership were
rarely a primary aim or outcome. Many sports centres and some arts centres provided space for voluntary organisations and some, indeed,
would find it difficult to survive without their rentals (cf. the opposite
examples of Fifty-Plus and W London CA). Almost all these facilities,
however, tended to be (and remain) professionally run and, in the case of
arts centres, to be devoted mainly to professional performances.

There was, of course, a rapid and substantial growth of voluntary
service organisations, especially though not solely for the young. Some
of these were based on national headquarters which ran local units with
varying degrees of independence. Others were sponsored by local CVSs
or rural development councils, and a small number were genuinely local
and autonomous, rather than just volunteer bureaux or organisations
managed by professionals and employing voluntary labour. The Home
Office Voluntary Service Unit was established in 1972 and delivered an
important stimulus to all such activity, while the Home Office Community Development Project, *pace* its name, tended to turn into community
work and, sometimes, attempts by professional and other community
workers and organisers to foster various kinds of change which seemed
desirable to them. All these multifarious activities attracted substantial
grants of public money to the organisation of volunteer labour, perhaps
especially in the wake of the Aves Committee's report (Aves, 1969). This
concerned itself mainly with the deployment of volunteers by the social
and health services under *their* control and for *their* purposes. The training of such volunteers in particular, but also the more general training
needs of the voluntary sector, were addressed by the first Gulbenkian
Report (1968). However, there was little national interest in or help for
local self-governing voluntary organisations.

Self-Help Groups

More significantly for our purposes, the 1960s and early 1970s also saw a
powerful acceleration in the development of self-help groups such as the
Pre-School Playgroups, or Alcoholics Anonymous and many others.
Whether local autonomous units of national associations or completely
free-standing, they asserted for the first time the capacity of local lay and
self-governing groups to play an effective part in work devoted to the al-

leviation of physical or psychological suffering or social deprivation. For some purposes they quickly proved more effective than professional services, rather than a poor substitute for them. It was realised that their impact was due to the fact that the unique experience of fellow-sufferers from a given condition could take effect in an autonomous and self-governing context. By excluding the instructing professional the groups offered a more effective because more acceptable transfer of knowledge, skills and attitudes through mutual support.

Over the years a framework of self-help networks sprang up in many parts of the country, often funded wholly or partly by the health service and jointly organised with CVSs. They offer a referral service to the public and the social and health services, vital but tactful assistance to individuals in the process of setting up new groups, and office services and publicity to new and established ones. They have learned, and maintain, the "hands-off" attitude which is essential if self-help is not to lapse into patronage. Our case studies of Widows SH, Macular SH, Arthritis SH, and Aekta SH are examples of self-help groups, and Bassetlaw CVS includes a self-help network, while the Retford study deals with the subject *passim*.

Linking Formal and Informal Learning ☞ 1960-1970s

During the same period the LEA adult education service evolved useful analogues to the self-help groups in its relationships with voluntary organisations. Most LA areas with effective services created schemes under various names which enabled and indeed encouraged LVOs to affiliate to the local adult education service. In return, and under a variety of advantageous financial arrangements, they could obtain both tuition (either *ad hoc* or on a permanent basis, such as the appointment of a conductor to a brass band or a coach to a club) and the free or cheap use of accommodation and facilities (including, e.g., classrooms, pitches or pools, or sewing machines). Similar facilities were available to voluntary groups in the youth service. The effect, more often than not, was to raise the standards of learning and performance and to make the organisation more attractive because better led, housed and equipped. As a result they also had a better survival rate.

There was also a less substantial but equally significant movement in the opposite direction. Where classes had continued for some years in adult education centres and achieved a good level of competence, they were encouraged to become independent of regular tuition and form themselves into affiliated clubs devoted to the practice of their subject, skill or art. They could continue to use the centre's accommodation and equipment, and might draw on advice or receive occasional tuition, but became autonomous practitioners and ran their own affairs. In a few rare instances LEA adult centres formed their student bodies into independent LVOs which could thus benefit under the Physical Training and Recreation regulations to provide modest additions to accommodation.

All these excellent developments harnessed voluntary responsibility and autonomy more productively to the processes of adult learning and its organisation in what was internationally known as the most effective system of general adult education anywhere. Their utility is not lessened by the unfortunate fact that they have fallen victim (as we found at Retford) to its virtual destruction over the last 20 years by successive governments.

More Recent Studies and Surveys

Starting long before such a prospect seemed credible, various attempts were made to at any rate find out what LVOs there were on the ground, though usually the objective remained linked to the formal system. Wilson and Ruddock's study (1959) was seminal in this respect and made adult educators throughout the country more eager to forge and exploit relationships with the voluntary sector. Some simply wanted to improve recruitment. Others pursued the vision of mutual support and joint planning outlined long ago by Marks (1949) and eventually developed in the 50-odd papers submitted to, and others produced by, the national research conference on *Planning and Co-operation to meet the Adult Education and Community Provision Needs of an Area,* which the DES ran in 1972. These papers were distributed nationally and raised awareness as well as stimulating action and further research.

The development of "community education" in the initially common sense of the term simply meant placing adult education and sometimes youth work within and under the authority of schools. It produced more claims than results, at least in relation to our topic. The only reliable accounts will be found in Mee and Wiltshire (1978), and Jennings (ND), while Elsdon (1989) tries to sort out the structural and terminological jungle around "community", the schools and the location of VOs and adult education.

Some other recent studies have been more germane to the project. They may have been stimulated by a variety of schemes and experiments which linked community work or even community action by adult educators, and gave some consideration to the educational processes which were involved. Jackson's original paper to the 1972 DES conference dealt magisterially with this topic and others, such as the principles and quality of learning involved. It was subsequently developed and formally published, and deserves to command continued attention (Jackson, 1973). Allen Tough's (1979) work stimulated wide-ranging approaches to such studies and Brookfield (1983) examined the incidence of adult learning in groups whose aims were not formally educational. Withnall (1990) usefully sorted out distinctions between formal and informal learning, though in relation to providers rather than learners. Darvill *et al.* (1988) concentrated on what may be learned from the process of volunteering, and Hall and Laplace (1983) and Withnall (1986) described the activities undertaken and the roles played by volunteers in a variety of voluntary and statutory contexts.

Closer Parallels

Two authors seem to us to be working in areas which are largely congruent with ours. They show greater awareness of the range and distribution of LVOs and are concerned with the nature of their activities and the exploration of their effects on individual members. As early as 1974–5 Elsey (1974, 1975) described a survey of 20 varied LVOs in which he studied not just the specific content-learning but the social development of members meeting their "expressive needs" through membership. He develops the theme further in Elsey (1993) and adds to it the suggestion that it is significant for the development of civil society. We would argue that the particular evidence he adduces does not, in fact, adequately support his argument, but that the evidence of our own case studies does. Both his recent and earlier papers are of importance to our own research context and repay study.

The other author whose work should be considered in relation to our own is Keith Percy. In his (1983) study he surveyed the educational activities of VOs in both a local and a regional sample. Clearly neither pretends to be comprehensive and the regional sample is less satisfactorily balanced because its source inevitably meant that only big fish were caught in the net. However, both samples develop the awareness of a variety of kinds and degrees of learning, and begin to indicate the true range of VOs. Both characteristics are more fully developed in his (1988) study. This survey identified 800 VOs in South Cumbria, Central Manchester and Preston. It made more sensitive distinctions between different kinds of both formal and informal learning than had been made hitherto and introduced a valuable categorisation of VOs. This was based on the two axes of a matrix, which were, respectively, (achievement / self-actualisation), and (altruism / self-esteem / affiliation).

Looking outwards from the VOs and their individual members to the impact which their learning and change make on local communities and society at large, their political tone and quality of life, we must return to our comments on works referred to earlier, especially Clarke (1990), Briggs and Macartney (1984), and to Batten's works. We also note the parallels to be found with the work of our colleagues Chris Duke (1992) and John Field (1990) on active citizenship. Our evidence is so consistent with them that it is easiest to say that of our 31 case studies and the Retford study only two do not strongly support it. Following on this persuasive range of evidence, three of the project's earlier publications (Elsdon, 1991a, 1991b, 1995) as well as the case studies themselves address the topic.

In conclusion it seems appropriate to return once more to some major recent findings. Chanan's (1992) report for the European Foundation for the Improvement of Living and Working Conditions is too rich and important for jejune comment here. Its concern with community action for welfare and other philanthropic ends is followed through in the context of an understanding of the *whole* voluntary field. Among other findings it stresses the need for the independence of VOs if they are to perform their proper civic functions, their development of local leader-

ship and active citizenship rather than mere consumership. It empha-
sises the need for public authorities to cherish and support the independence of groups which the community needs. Core funding was
found to be crucial in this, and contract funding (except on a small scale
and at the discretion of the organisation) destructive of both voluntary
service and proper organisational objectives. In these and very many
other areas its findings run parallel to some of ours, and they are mutually supportive.

We have found ourselves less in sympathy with *some* of the findings
of Knight (1993). Judging by our own evidence, his conclusions appear to
be based on a problematic definition, and they seem to rest on a flawed
picture of the overall size, characteristics and distribution of the total
range of voluntary organisations in Britain. Moreover, his policy recom-
mendations do not seem to us to be supported by his own evidence.
However, his evidence of the effects of contracting out public services to
VOs, and of the contract culture upon these, is more substantial than
ours from Bassetlaw CVS, the Settlement, UIMWO and the Retford
study, and entirely convincing.

We return to Chanan's *Taken for Granted* (1991), which, although a
critical response to a political party's policy document, should be regarded as an independent summary statement in its own right; in its
own words it "is about national policy towards the voluntary and community sector". It acknowledges that "Independent local community
groups are the largest and least-funded part of the voluntary sector.
They arise from community activity, not from national voluntary organisations." In the compass of a mere 20 pages Chanan describes and de-
fines the sector, its organisations and activities, sets out appropriate
relationships with umbrella bodies, local and central government, clari-
fies the problems and consequences of funding, and the link between
voluntary responsibility and citizenship. We do not find ourselves in
agreement with every detail of the document, but regard it as the best we
know and essential reading for anyone concerned with the voluntary
field.

This chapter must end with what can hardly be more than leading
questions. We have found ourselves in sympathy most of all with some
of the recent contributions. These could be said to initiate radically different approaches to the subject. Does this switch echo a major change of
balance in the voluntary sector itself? LVOs have always existed, but is it
not true that they have come much more to the fore as their range of
complexity and content grew? Are we perhaps becoming aware of a
secular change in the balance of voluntaryism, away from nineteenth-
century emphases on the duty of relief and service, and towards a more
egalitarian and humanist understanding both of the community and of
interest communities within it?

Chapter 3

Sources, Patterns and an Approximate Model

This book seeks to describe LVOs only in so far as description aids its main aim, to discover what learning and change LVOs stimulate in their members, and how these outcomes affect others and the community at large. It is therefore necessary to start with description, to trace the relationship of what we have studied to the VO picture as a whole, and to introduce some main aspects of our analysis, including ways in which we shall categorise LVOs. This chapter begins by describing briefly the 31 LVOs of which case studies have been made. For this purpose it will group them according to their organisational objectives. It will then adduce the findings of a comparison between the case studies and the Retford locality study, and show that the two investigations together mirror, albeit in soft focus, by far the greater part of the whole territory of voluntary organisations. On that basis some national generalisations will be hazarded about LVOs and their members.

The Case Studies

The sample of LVOs chosen for the case studies represents the typology with its matrix of 343 descriptors. The interview programme confirmed the expectation that both organisational and personal objectives would almost always be both multiple, and stratified, as shown by the different main and subsidiary matrix entries. It would therefore be productive to match and contrast these entries with one another descriptively, integrating statistics from all three data bases to deepen the perspective, in order to arrive at some understanding of the motives and characteristics of both members and organisations. Some of the outcomes are described in Chapters 4 and 5; far more had to be excluded because not directly relevant to this report. All the materials are available, in raw form, in the project's archive.

The case studies are representative in another way which is important, though there will be no further occasion to refer to it. The interviews conducted for them with 831 individuals represent, in general terms, a total membership in these particular organisations which exceeds 8,000 individuals. Moreover, the 343 descriptors exemplified by the selection mean that the case studies illustrate not just organisational and personal objectives but various combinations of the size, funding, staffing and structure of LVOs, as well as their geographical, demographic, social, ethnic and gender mixes and distribution. Together they therefore present a broad-brush picture of what LVOs and their members in Britain are like. They are *not* an attempt to quantify different or-

ganisations and memberships nationally. The very large general trawl at
Retford does, however, permit an attempt at projecting overall *proportions* of different kinds of organisations and their memberships. This will
follow the mapping of LVOs on the basis of the case studies.

The mapping process begins by placing and briefly describing the individual case studies within a typology based upon primary organisational objectives, i.e. the headings of the seven vertical columns of the
matrix.

1. Social Service, Community Development, Umbrella Bodies

The objectives in this heading are characteristic of community associations and intermediary groups, most of which shelter numbers of smaller
groups. They include a growing number of local churches, as shown by
the Retford study, though none are included in the case study sample.
Some smaller organisations devoted to specific objectives also fall into
this group.

The Bassetlaw CVS is an example of a medium-sized (cf. Glossary)
intermediary group which engages in direct work of its own, facilitates
the establishment and functioning of other groups, and forms an interactive network with them and with other local spheres of activity and their
personnel, including local public services, local government, business,
the professions, and other funding bodies. All are represented in its
membership and its elective structures. It is substantially funded, from
public sources in particular, and has paid professional and other staff, as
well as attracting voluntary service.

The Settlement, an inner-city London one, fosters its own and a number of independent and semi-independent activities and organisations
which respond to the needs of the surrounding population. Its individual membership, though in the large category, is limited by financial resources and especially by a very small LA grant. Much of its work is
undertaken by volunteer members, some of whom may become employed at times for specific tasks. The main organisational emphasis is on
social service, adult basic education and community development, advocacy and representation, in an area with a large and diverse ethnic minority population and severe problems. The energy necessarily
expended by senior staff on fund raising inevitably limits that which is
available for work more relevant to the organisation's purpose.

A contrast is provided by the suburban W London CA. This, too, is
an umbrella for many activities, but mostly in the capacity of a landlord
letting out space. Taking into account the members of organisations using the building, it is large. The main emphasis is on sport, leisure interests and activities which contribute to the financial viability of the
Association, recently turned into a Limited Company. Links with, and
development work within, the local community have been neglected in
recent years and the original purposes of a community association have
become obscured.

The fourth in this group, Ingleton CA, is a large umbrella organisation in a Northern rural setting. With a tiny staff and relatively little external funding, it embraces and provides facilities for a wide range of

community groups, community and economic development, educational activities and sport, arising from the needs and enthusiasms of local people. The association maintains its original purpose and vigour, and its influence permeates the life of the community.

Some organisations in this group have more specific service objectives. The Volunteer Drivers are a very small group. Its members use their own cars to offer transport to people who would otherwise find travel to maintain their interests and reach hospitals and other facilities difficult. It is more like a volunteer employing agency and illustrates the fine boundary between this and an LVO. The Rotary Club, another small group, has service to the community as its main objective. It gives financial help, and members' and their wives' time, to some local good causes while providing members and their families with a much appreciated social life. The Playgroup, also small, provides in a village setting care and education for under-fives and support for their mothers through the often isolating and stressful early years of motherhood.

Ujima is one of two case studies of LVOs in an ethnic minority, in this case the African-Caribbean community. A small organisation offering advice and information, it was well-staffed for its size and relied wholly on LA funding at the time of our study. It was active especially among young people in helping with careers advice and job applications.

The unpublished study of UIMWO examined a long-established organisation which is now principally engaged in social and welfare services delivered by professionals under contract to statutory bodies. Little membership or volunteer involvement seemed to be apparent.

2. Advocacy

Many LVOs carry out advocacy on behalf of members or their cause. Three case study organisations, however, have advocacy as their primary objective. The Residents' Association stands for tenants' and residents' rights in general and promotes improvements to the local environment. The PTA is concerned with the education and well-being of children and other users of their community school, and the mobilisation of parent support. Both have large potential memberships but few active members. Both are run by volunteers, the PTA with some LEA help. Both seek to raise the ability of members to deal with professionals and administrators who have power over the provision of services.

The Wildlife Trust is one of the very many LVOs which act as advocates for the rural environment and its fauna and flora. A large and active group, it operates wholly through the efforts of volunteers among its membership and receives no external funding. It is concerned with the protection and management of wild life habitats and the ecology of ancient woodlands and meadows. Many volunteer hours are spent in practical work such as coppicing and clearing ditches.

3. Health Education, Mutual Support, Care

A number of groups had one or more of these as subsidiary objectives but self-help groups have them as their raison d'être. They have proliferated to such an extent over the past decade or more that the inclusion of several seemed appropriate. Macular SH, Patients' Support and Arthritis SH were all founded and supported with the assistance of Bassetlaw CVS and its Self-Help Network. The first two are small, and Arthritis SH medium-sized with over 80 members. All are typical of the genre in that their members are (or were, in one of them) themselves sufferers from the conditions which the groups are aiming to alleviate by mutual support. None of these groups has paid staff, but all had received start-up grants and are continuing to receive help in kind. Because of the incidence of macular disease and arthritis most members of these two groups are over retirement age. In the third, former patients are giving voluntary support to those struggling to recover from mental illness.

Aekta SH is the second example of a minority ethnic LVO, this time from the Asian community. A small self-help group with one worker provided by external funding, it brings together into a sympathetic cultural setting people who care for sick and disabled relatives at home.

Case study 8 (Widows SH) is also a self-help group, but will be described under its primary objective of provision for women.

4. Physical Activity

Making contact with groups whose main objective was physical activity proved difficult because those dedicated to a single sport were most absorbed in their activity and proved least open to communication with outsiders. Sport figures largely in both community associations, and representatives of judo, boxing, ordinary and five-a-side football, badminton, bowls, tennis, and cricket were interviewed. The primary organisational purpose of Mountain Rescue is evidently physical although members have to acquire and maintain a wide range of other motivation and skills for their task. It is medium-sized.

Fifty-Plus took the researchers into the North West of England to a very large LVO with an elderly membership, whose objectives centre mainly on physical activities. With no paid staff or any form of external support the group is responsible for 28 regular weekly activities for a membership of over 1,500. All leadership, coaching and organisation are undertaken by volunteers from among the members. Most of these are also part of informal networks meeting outside the formal activities to provide mutual support and friendship. Many of the members are involved in voluntary service to other organisations, particularly for the elderly.

5. Specific Interests and Hobbies

This group of objectives includes the pursuit, through LVOs, of education and the arts in a purposeful and more or less structured way, as well as societies which cater for a single interest. Thus two local Workers' Educational Association branches (S Wales and Kelvedon), the first only nominally medium-sized and the second on the borderline between this and small, have the provision of classes in the liberal tradition of adult education as their main objective. One is successful in providing intellectual and social stimulation for its members, and links them with other organisations with similar objectives and with public service. The Guildhouse, founded as a voluntary adult education centre almost 70 years ago, bears witness to the strength of voluntaryism in adult education: it survives without paid professional leadership, with exiguous paid office help and only very slight external funding in proportion to the large size of its membership and educational programme. In addition to its intellectual and social significance to generations of members it has been the wellspring of other flourishing civic and arts groups in the town.

Two further LVOs with educational objectives (the NWR and WI Groups) will be described under their primary objective of provision for women.

Three case studies concern LVOs whose main objectives are devoted to aspects of the arts. The Arts Centre, a large organisation, houses a wide range and large volume of activities which are well supported by its catchment population, and acts as an umbrella to many others. With a small professional staff and meagre funding it relies on very large amounts of voluntary service for the vigour and variety of its activities. The Singers are a small group of dedicated perfectionists whose performances are enjoyed by discerning audiences regionally and in their twin area in Germany. The Writers' Workshop, the sole case study from Scotland, is a small group of individualists who join together in their love of poetry and Scottish culture. Both are tightly coherent groups of people dedicated to their creative purpose, and carrying on their work without any external funding and little or no help in kind.

Four further case studies cover very different interests or hobbies as their main objectives: archaeology, steam railways, allotment gardening and pigeon racing. The Railway Trust's membership is very large, and that of the Gardeners substantial; the other two fall into the medium category as defined in the Glossary. All four illustrate the way in which all so-called "hobbies", if taken seriously, involve the acquisition of substantial and often complex and varied areas of knowledge as well as practical skills and personal attitudes. The Railway Trust, with 1,500 members and some 20 paid staff, is by far the largest and most complex. Its operations have been developed to such a size that it would be straying into the category of non-profit making firms were it not for the members' enormous input of voluntary time and enthusiasm in all aspects of its activities (cf. Stewart *et al.*, pp. 203–7). These cater for many thousands of visitors annually. Similar levels of dedication, involvement and regular and demanding voluntary work, though on a smaller scale, are implicit in the other three groups, all of which mediate substantial and varied knowledge bases and require their continual development for successful performance.

6. Sociability

Sociability as a main objective is usually assumed to characterise passive social or welfare clubs or bingo. The case study sample did not include a group which had this as its primary objective, though it featured as a strong subsidiary one in many of the LVOs which were studied. It is important to distinguish between sociability as an organisational objective and as a personal one. Its significance as a personal objective to members of LVOs in all categories will be examined in Chapter 5.

7. Provision for Women

As an objective, provision for women differs from the others because it is about a target, not content. It was separated out in the first instance in order to ensure adequate attention to women's organisations. Three were included. The Derby Branch of the National Association of Widows is a self-help group whose objective is specified in its name. It provides support, information and advice in a sympathetic social setting. Two other women's groups figure under this primary objective, but have educational interests and hobbies as extremely strong subsidiaries. They are the small "Silverbridge" NWR Group and the medium-sized Sibsey WI. Both are autonomous local groups of long-established women's organisations which meet the needs and interests of women and act as advocates for them. In both, learning activities are of prime importance, but they are presented informally, and sociability as an objective ranks alongside education. None of these three women's organisations has any paid staff, nor are they receiving help in cash or kind; they flourish through the enthusiasm and commitment of their members. Individuals in each of the last two provide very active support and commitment to other LVOs.

The Retford Locality Study

The reasons for including a locality study of Retford (population 20,679 in 1991) were explained in Chapter 1. Its findings about objectives and motives, interaction and networking contribute to subsequent chapters. In the present context the information may be used for a different purpose, as a basis for an approximate model of the distribution of British VOs in general. The Retford data base rests on returns and interviews from, altogether, 101 organisations, compared with 335 which were known to exist. At least a further 115 could be identified, and raise the known total to 450.

No doubt the limited response introduced distortions, and some of these, at least, are known and can be taken into account. Thus, in the "Advocacy" category, none of the trade unions and only one small political organisation are represented, while there was a high return from churches and traditional philanthropic organisations. Under "practical interests" women's sport is under-represented compared with men's, because none of the Keep Fit and similar organisations responded. In general terms, however, the Retford statistics enable us to extrapolate certain total national *estimates*, which cannot be derived from the case study sample.

Thus the minimum of 450 voluntary organisations of all kinds at Retford, or 1:46 to the population, would scale up to about 1.3 million nationally. This is within range of but very reasonably less than Ingleton's probably exceptional 1:39.5 or 1.5 millions. The total membership recorded for the Retford groups which disclosed this information was 6,630, divided almost equally between women (3,545) and men (3,085). This is surprising in itself, since it had been generally assumed (perhaps by comparison with experience in adult education) that women would form at least two-thirds of the total. Scaled up to the 450 minimum for the town this comes to 29,540 memberships, equivalent to 143% of its population – 81.5 millions if scaled up to a national total. Two qualifying factors must, however, be stressed at once.

One is that the 101 organisations which responded quite possibly included a high proportion of the larger LVOs. The other factor is the considerable proportion of LVO members who belong to more than one organisation. Bearing in mind known participation rates (cf. pp. 39, 89–92 below), what can be said with some degree of confidence is that an overwhelming majority of the adult population belongs to at least one LVO, and a high proportion of these to more than one. Set alongside the Volunteer Centre's (1991) 23 millions total of those volunteering their services (if only to rattle a tin once a year) and its 100 million hours of voluntary activity per week, these figures seem entirely realistic.

An Approximate Model

Retford also provides us with a model estimate of the breakdown of the presumed total of about 1.3 millions of voluntary organisations, their members, and their characteristics. There seems to be no reason why the Retford percentages, on which the following graphs and tables are based, should not form a possible basis for a first attempt at projecting national estimates.

Diagram 1: Retford: percentages of organisations by organisational objectives and percentages of members by the same (cp. Table 1, Appendix 4)

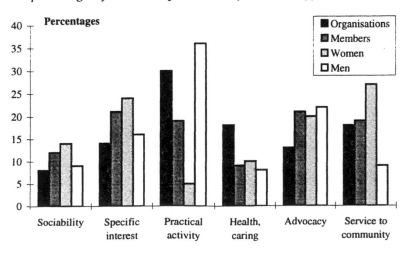

In an ancient market town with a strong middle class the local branches of the established philanthropic agencies are certainly not under-represented. Almost certainly 70% of them responded to the postal questionnaire. This was a far better response rate than the overall one of 22%. Proportionately, the big philanthropic VOs are thus over-represented in the Retford sample. Nevertheless, if they and their memberships are extracted from it, they make up only 7% of organisations and 9% of members (13% of women and 4% of men). This reinforces our estimate elsewhere (paralleled by Chanan, 1991) that this, the best-known segment of all the voluntary organisations, represents less than 10% of the total.

Even without taking account of the major charities, some interesting contrasts emerge from the breakdown of objectives and memberships. Women are much more strongly represented in public service (unless the absence of unions and political parties makes this deceptive), but the sexes are almost equal in health and caring, and advocacy. Both groups of specific interests together, i.e. practical, sporting, intellectual, arts and the rest, scored 44% of organisations and 40% of members. Specific interests therefore emerge as by far the strongest area. Within this, however, there are very marked differences between practical and other interests and women's and men's participation. If women's sport were more adequately represented this contrast would be reduced by raising the relative importance of practical, as opposed to other, activities, and of women as opposed to men. Nevertheless the differences would remain highly significant.

Specific interest organisations tend to be small or medium-sized, and their predominance is therefore reflected in the breakdown of organisational size:

Diagram 2: Retford: small, medium and large organisations by percentage

Membership % (N=96)
0-29	52
30-99	33
100+	15

Specialist predominance is also reflected in the contrast between organisations which specialise in a particular area of activity or interest, and those which cover a variety of them. The former would include, for instance, football clubs or dramatic and other specialist societies but not umbrella organisations such as a sports centre, a CVS, an arts centre, or other generalist organisations like a Women's Institute or a civic society. Specialist organisations form 66% of the total and generalists the balance of 34%.

The link between objectives or activities and the typical "stance" of organisations is more problematical. In Chapter 7 it is suggested that one way in which organisations may be categorised is by their current stance. This may be either "dynamic" (e.g. developing, engaged in constructive change), or "static" (unchanging, on a plateau of activity), or divergent (having undergone or currently undergoing changes which are negative in relation to the organisation's objectives). The static category includes two broad types. The larger consists of organisations which are satisfactorily meeting their objectives and only have to maintain themselves in their current stance to continue successful. The smaller includes those whose development has been arrested in such a manner that they show signs of declining into the divergent category.

It will be realised that a high proportion of specialist activities – for example a hockey team, an allotment society or a self-help group – will go through a dynamic phase while they establish themselves, but that healthy stasis must be their long-term objective. Conversely generalist activities such as umbrella groups, public or social service organisations and those specialists whose activity requires continually expanding learning or change (e.g. Mountain Rescue, the Railway Trust) have to maintain their dynamism to remain healthy.

These explanations must be borne in mind when considering the following breakdown:

Diagram 3: Typical stance of Retford organisations by percentages

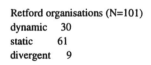

Retford organisations (N=101)
dynamic   30
static   61
divergent   9

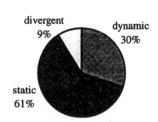

However, in the Retford sample six, or 10%, of the static organisations, were showing an obvious tendency to move into the divergent category. If this is taken into account then the distribution changes to 30, 55 and 15%. Given a detailed consideration of all the actual responses, these percentages suggest interesting conclusions about the overall state of voluntary organisations. As many as 85% appear to be in good heart. They include roughly equal proportions of specialist and generalist organisations. It needs to be borne in mind, however, that this perception rests on a 22% response. It is more than possible that the proportion of weak organisations may have been higher among the non-respondents. Some of the percentages into which organisational objectives break down are too small for significant conclusions to be drawn. However, two-thirds of the 9% in the divergent category are from the organisations which pursue community service and health and caring as their objectives, and two-thirds of these are local branches of national philanthropic charities or agencies. If the six static groups with notably regressive characteristics are added, then the proportion of big welfare organisations remains the same. This suggests that the 7% of voluntary organisations which are best known, best staffed and funded, could also include two-thirds of *all* those organisations locally which are in the least healthy state. Studies by Knight (1993) and the Volunteer Centre (1991) findings, it will be recalled, showed these to have difficulty in maintaining their volunteer forces. There are very probable links between these findings and the fact that these organisations are centralised, with little or no very effective local democracy, and that their paid staff were appointed by centralised hierarchies. Questions of constitution, structure and relationships arise which are addressed more particularly in Chapter 9.

A further criterion for categorising LVOs by their objectives is whether they are inward- or outward-looking, or mostly sociable. At only 8% the purely sociable group is very small and it can, logically, be treated as belonging to the inward category. The actual distribution is:

Diagram 4: Retford: inward- and outward-looking organisations (N=101)

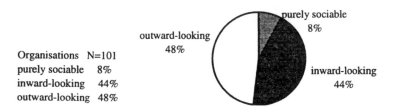

Organisations   N=101
purely sociable   8%
inward-looking   44%
outward-looking   48%

The criterion is whether an organisation's activities are directed solely or primarily to satisfying the needs or interests of its members, or primarily those of others, or the general public. The Railway Trust, for instance, exists primarily for the interest, pleasure and amusement of its members and thus looks inward upon itself. The pleasure of the large number of paying visitors is only a necessary by-product. On the other hand, the W London CA may have cut itself off from its local community in practice. However, its organisational objective is to serve the local community, and thus to look outward beyond its own membership. It looked at first as if this division was not going to be particularly productive of new insights. It appeared to be fairly close to the specialist–generalist one, and some of the logically necessary allocations (e.g. the

Residents' Association and the WI Group as inward and Rotary and UIMWO as outward) seemed nonsensical.

However, there is another way in which this division links up usefully with others. Purely sociable organisations (i.e. the extreme end of the inward spectrum) are least likely to have links with other organisations or with the public sector – probably because they are largely self-sufficient. Outward-looking organisations tend to have more links with others and with the public, the economic and the professional sectors, mainly in connection with resources provided or required by them. Outward-looking groups also tend to be distinctly larger, to have more and closer links of every kind, and also to have paid staff. The reason is that they include a high proportion of those which provide services to clients or members. This often requires the intervention of paid staff, whose salaries usually have to be met from grant-aid.

The case studies and the Retford exercise differ in content. A number of details are missing from the Retford information, but well documented in the case studies. However, on comparison the general characteristics derived from the Retford data base and those from the case studies proved reasonably consistent in the range of objectives, variety of activities, the preponderance of specialist organisations, organisational structure and variations in size and funding. This justifies using the data bases in conjunction with each other, and greatly extends the *generally* descriptive material which is available. It also enhances the degree of confidence in the representative function of the case study sample.

It follows therefore that we are able to add the following statistics, each of them expressed as percentages of the total of 522 members with known TEA:

Diagram 5: Terminal education ages of members (%)

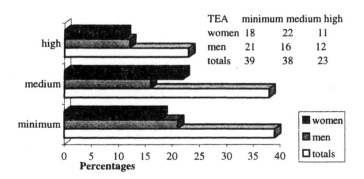

TEA	minimum	medium	high
women	18	22	11
men	21	16	12
totals	39	38	23

Given the degree of bias towards successful LVOs in the sample, one would expect a distribution skewed away from the low and towards the high end of the spectrum of TEA. In fact, the proportion of those with a minimum TEA (with similar proportions of women and men) is considerably higher than would be expected in a sample which has been selected in this way. We shall return to this topic in Chapter 5. However, the factors which may have caused the TEAs to be less skewed than expected are also likely to be responsible for a number of other general outcomes. Among these the rate of participation (cf. Glossary) in activities, and the proportion of those who assume responsibility within organisations, are particularly surprising. The factors which affect the distribution of TEA are likely to be partly responsible.

The very high general rate of participation in voluntary activities has been reported above (cf. p. 33). Information from the questionnaire data base (N=157, being 103 women and 54 men) shows how participation by LVO members develops over time, and reveals interesting differences between the sexes:

Diagram 6: Percentage changes in rate of participation over time (N=157)

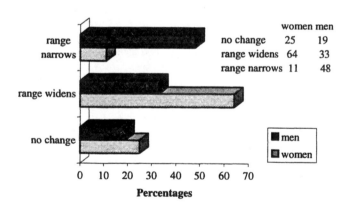

	women	men
no change	25	19
range widens	64	33
range narrows	11	48

When (in Chapters 6 and 7) the pervasive differences between specialist and generalist LVOs are discussed, it will be noted that a majority of men have a tendency to gravitate toward the former and a majority of women toward the latter. These opposed tendencies are here reflected in highly significant proportions of women whose interests and participation expand, while those of a smaller but still highly significant proportion of men tend to home in on some special target.

Voluntary Responsibility

Finally, the research casts some light on the proportion of people who assume voluntary responsibility. Here again the degree of selectiveness in the main sample is bound to exaggerate the overall average, which is, indeed, astonishing. 39% of the case study sample (equivalent to almost 17 millions of the adult population) serve as officers, committee members or in some other responsible post in their LVO. There is no significant difference between women (35%) and men (43%) in this respect. We know from partial returns that, on average, a similar percentage discharged responsibilities in other organisations, including anything from other LVOs to elective public offices, but excluding occupational responsibilities. If half the projected total of service to other bodies is deducted as overlap we are still left with a total of 25 million individuals serving their own organisations. This is 56% of the UK population over the age of 18.

Such figures sound impossible. Yet, even if the sampling distortion were so great as to necessitate halving them, we are still left with a formidable total of 12 million women and men *currently* involved in running at least 1.3 million small democracies throughout the country. It is indeed a solemn thought, one to which we shall recur more particularly in Chapters 8 and 10.

The use of the three data bases enables a large number of increasingly fascinating and potentially important discoveries to be made, such as relationships between learning objectives, size, external funding, staffing and interaction between organisations, and many more. It becomes obvious that generalist organisations tend to have more links with others and with the public sector than specialist ones. They influence the quality of life of their area more directly through personal participation, the transmission of ideas, through advocacy and other forms of pressure. The specialists, on the other hand, tend to do so to no less effect but indirectly through their various activities, or through the provision of particular material facilities and opportunities for participation. Key organisations – especially umbrella or intermediary – turn up regularly at nodal points of networks. So do particular individual generalist organisations. In our Retford and main samples civic societies, the Inner Wheel or a Women's Institute were obvious but by no means isolated examples. Here again the predominance of women should be noted. Key individuals with multiple links play a similar part on a more intimate scale and their activities are illustrated in Reynolds *et al.* (1994), p. 25f.

These are no more than examples of a very large quantity of descriptive material obtained directly from individuals and organisations, and confirmed by independent observers. Only some of it, which relates directly to our topic of learning and change, will be used in the following chapters. All of it is deposited among our archive material to await detailed exploration.

Before we turn to the project's main findings it may be useful to highlight a few early conclusions:

- There is a very large number of VOs of all kinds. More than 90% of them are local. The best known national bodies appear to represent less than 10% of organisations and members.

- Well over half the adult population belongs to LVOs and the great majority of them to more than one. Women and men are equally active but differ noticeably in the kinds of organisations which they tend to join.

- Organisations devoted to specific personal interests (practical, sporting, intellectual and the arts) are the strongest single area with over two-fifths of organisations and members.

- Almost all LVOs are democratic and possibly as many as 39% of members bear some kind of elected responsibility in them. As many as 56% of the United Kingdom's adult population over the age of 18 seem to be serving their own organisations in some capacity or other.

- It is possible to categorise LVOs in a number of ways for the purposes of analysis. Those which will be used most are:

  - specialist – generalist – mostly sociable
  - inward-looking – outward-looking
  - dynamic – static – divergent.

- Personal characteristics of members, such as age, sex and terminal education age, and group characteristics such as size and staffing, and stated and perceived objectives and outcomes, relate variously to the categories above.

Chapter 4

Objectives and Outcomes

Incongruence and its Causes

Following the outlines of the background and general territory of our research, we are now able to begin the task of presenting our main findings. We do so by continuing, for the time being, to move from more generic and external areas of analysis towards the centre of individual learning and change. This will be the subject of the following chapter. To prepare for it, however, it is fruitful to compare the aims and learning objectives pursued by organisations, and the objectives and outcomes or benefits as reported by their members. In the light of a review of our case studies and interview records, our essential finding here is that organisational objectives and member outcomes were incongruent (in the value-free geometrical sense), that the incongruence was universal, and that, while differing in degree, it was rarely less than striking. It is the nature and causes of these incongruences, and of their differences in degree, which are of interest.

The intentions and objectives of organisations are usually clear from their constitutions. If they are informal, purpose is mostly implicit in their titles. There can be little doubt about the objectives of a self-help group, a local football league, a chamber choir, or a boxing club. Where objectives are more complex, as in the case of a community association, a CVS, a railway preservation society or a women's discussion group, they are usually laid down in a document and were well known to our respondents. It is on the basis of this range of information, and with the help of methods and findings from the Retford study, that we were able to suggest a tentative model as outlined in the preceding chapter, and to group organisations together according to their objectives in a variety of ways. The most obvious of these proved to be continua, such as from specialist to generalist, from inward- to outward-looking or from altruistic to personal. A rather more fruitful way of expressing these distinctions is to place groups, roughly, since measurement is here impracticable, in a simple diagram which expresses their characteristics impressionistically. Some examples illustrate this:

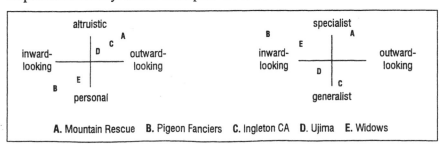

A. Mountain Rescue   B. Pigeon Fanciers   C. Ingleton CA   D. Ujima   E. Widows

A general picture of the distribution of organisational objectives at Retford and possibly nationally has been sketched in the preceding chapter. Our task here is to draw attention to what turned out to be the incongruence between these objectives and the motives and outcomes which members described for us. This varied in degree both individually and by organisations, but was always notable. Moreover, it could vary not only as part of the snapshot picture produced by case study interviews and questionnaire returns, but even more if considered longitudinally over an extended period of membership with the help of the questionnaire returns and the fullest interviews. Thus several of the Ingleton CA respondents' main (but by no means sole) motives and outcomes had initially echoed those of this mainly generalist and outward-looking organisation during its earlier years. As they retired and aged, personal and inward-looking motives and benefits tended to become more important, and, for some, specialised and inward-looking interests tended to take precedence.

It will be easiest to start this survey of incongruence where that characteristic is least pronounced.The Pigeon Fanciers exist primarily to provide facilities for competition between their members and to control the manner in which this is conducted. This involves a fundamental ambiguity: members *have to* co-operate if competition between them is to take place. They are much involved in and stimulated by competitive activities. Except for initial help to new members there is little else by way of benefits that arises from the process of membership. The major satisfactions and learnings arising from pigeon fancying were reported to centre round the personal and indeed secretive study and care of birds, their breeding, training and racing. The personal outcomes of *group* membership as such were limited except for the excitement of the races, and very nearly congruent with the organisational objectives.

This is the extreme and least incongruent case among the 31. It appears to be significant that it is an inward-looking organisation. In our search for causes it seemed best to rank organisations in the order of this variance from the virtual congruence of the Pigeon Fanciers to the most markedly opposite examples. For maximum clarity in distinguishing degrees of incongruence we then drew a borderline to separate out the 11 organisations where it was most strongly marked, i.e. a minority:

- the NWR Group, Ingleton CA, the Arts Centre, the WI Group, Rotary, Patients' Support, Archaeologists, Singers, Fifty-Plus, the Settlement and Mountain Rescue.

In the remaining majority group of 20 organisations incongruence ranged from what was still substantial to moderate and slight.

Beginning with the slight to moderate cases, and in no particular order, we tried to assign possible reasons for relatively slight differences between organisational objectives and personal outcomes. The Guildhouse has objectives which are particularly broad and inclusive; for instance, a strong element of social as well as academic learning is here an overt aim. A wide range of member objectives can thus be accommodated within the organisational ones. Ujima, on the other hand, had such limited outcomes that little variation from the organisational objectives could be expected. Self-help groups of all kinds and other specialists such as the Wildlife Trust had objectives which were either precisely defined or carefully aimed and inclusive, or both. Some groups (such as Rotary or the S Wales WEA Branch) were either narrowly limited or unsuccessful and thus unlikely to stimulate member objectives or outcomes much beyond those of the organisation. Some, such as Aekta SH, were too new for their members to have yet discovered their full potential.

All these examples exhibit relatively slight differences between organisational objectives and member outcomes, yet they allow of a varied range of possible diagnoses. As well as those already suggested, slight incongruence in the PTA reflects weaknesses in the organisation. Elsewhere, as in the Volunteer Drivers, aspirations are modest and the goal is attained. The diagnoses differ widely; nevertheless the division into strongly and moderately to weakly incongruent groups begins to suggest some likely conclusions if we look for common characteristics.

In the weakly incongruent group all the organisations except Ijima belong to the inward-looking category, and the inward-looking organisations were found to be three times as likely to be only moderately or slightly incongruent. This observation may be linked with the quite specific objectives of many inward-looking groups. Their members were interested primarily in maintaining or developing a particular interest in accordance with the organisational objectives. Their focus may therefore be more strongly directed. There is also a marked difference between women's and men's membership of strongly incongruent LVOs. Over two-fifths of women belong to them but only just over a quarter of men.

Since the reasons for all these incongruences differ so widely between organisations they cannot lie solely in the fact that these organisations are inward-looking. If we consider the 11 outward-looking ones we find that six of them (Ingleton CA, Arts Centre, Rotary, Patients' Support, Settlement and Mountain Rescue) coincide with the (deliberately restricted) strongly incongruent category of 11 LVOs which have just been listed. The numbers are too small to talk of "significance", but they are suggestive. Of these six organisations Rotary enjoys only limited success in its main objective, but the social life of the organisation has been so successful as to overtake it. All the other five (Ingleton CA, Arts Centre, Settlement, Patients' Support, and Mountain Rescue) are distinguished by the extraordinary demands they make on the committed involvement of their members and the range of learning and personal development required if these are to be able to support the organisation's objectives. These six are by no means the only ones among the 31 of which this is true, but they point towards a possible line of reasoning.

The division of strongly incongruent LVOs into specialists and generalists reveals highly significant differences between the membership of men and women. Of the 11 strongly incongruent LVOs, the NWR Group, Ingleton CA, the Arts Centre, the WI Group, Rotary, Fifty-Plus and the Settlement are generalist. Just over one-third of all the members interviewed are in strongly incongruent groups, and 70% of these (90 women and 40 men) are in generalist groups. Members with minimum TEAs, particularly men, are much more likely to be found in specialist LVOs than those with longer first cycle education. Over half of all men but just over one-third of women are in moderate to weakly incongruent organisations which are also specialist. These include the Railway Trust, Gardeners and Pigeon Fanciers, i.e. practical groups with a heavy male preponderance.

It is thus possible to state that, in general:

- members of generalist groups are very much more likely to have and to further develop a wide range of interests beyond the group's immediate objectives, while members of specialist groups, though sharing this tendency, do so to a far lesser extent
- women display evidence of intellectual and cultural adventurousness to a much higher degree than men, whose interests are more linear and focused, especially upon practical activities
- there is evidence that those whose education has been least privileged *tend to have* (we shall discover significant exceptions) a narrower range of interests which are more congruent with their organisation's objectives.

This line of argument can be developed further by comparing the strongly incongruent groups and the rest according to whether the terminal education ages (TEA) of their members are, on balance, low, middling, or high. It will be recalled that of the total member sample whose TEA was known (522), 205 (94 women, 111 men) had received whatever had been the minimum first cycle education when they left school. When the figures for TEA are grouped under high and moderate to weakly incongruent LVOs, a very different and highly significant distribution emerges. This shows almost three times as many members with minimum TEA in moderate to weakly incongruent groups as in strong ones. In the educationally most privileged group, however, there were only one-third more in the least than the most incongruent organisations. A higher proportion of women than men are in strongly incongruent groups, and only one in seven of men with minimum TEA is to be found there, compared with almost two-fifths of other men:

Diagram 7: Incongruence and TEA (cp. Table 2, Appendix 4)

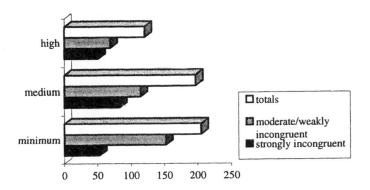

What emerges strongly and consistently is that:

- members of moderate or weakly incongruent LVOs with
  minimum TEA emphasise specific and, particularly, practical
  interests and immediate sources of enjoyment much more than
  others.

Cause and effect are hard to distinguish in these matters, but it looks as if the educationally more privileged are also likely to benefit from membership along a broader front than the majority, and that a higher proportion of them contribute widely and energetically to the content of an organisation's activity. The study of individual learning and change in the next chapter will reinforce this evidence, but it will also reveal important exceptions to the rule.

In general, however, the available evidence suggests that the demands which active involvement in the organisation makes upon members are the most important cause of incongruence between organisational objectives and member objectives and outcomes. Moreover it seems likely that the degree of intensity of this involvement at least influences and possibly determines that of the incongruence. The sources of these demands may vary widely and include, e.g., leadership as well as other influences and forms of organisational momentum.

The evidence about incongruence which has been outlined here rests only on our 31 case studies. While these are representative of the *kinds* of LVOs in existence they are not a representative sample. The Retford statistics of incongruence between organisational objectives and member objectives and benefits offer a closer approach. In the first instance it was found there that most organisations assumed their members' objectives and outcomes were either the same, or very close to, the organisation's objectives. This was far from the truth. If objectives and benefits are conflated into the three general categories (purely or almost purely sociable; inward-looking, which includes special interests and practical, including sporting, activities; and outward-looking, which includes health, caring, community service and advocacy), then the incongruences become amply clear. There is equilibrium over the inward-looking group, but sociable motives are more than three times higher among members than the organisations assume. On the other hand only three-fifths of the members whom organisations believe to have outward-looking motives do so in fact.

Diagram 8: Retford: Organisations' objectives and member outcomes compared (N=101)

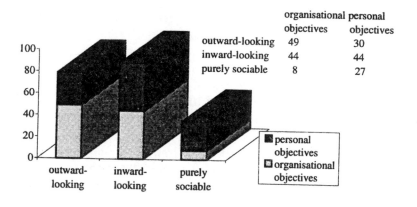

	organisational objectives	personal objectives
outward-looking	49	30
inward-looking	44	44
purely sociable	8	27

The Nature of Incongruence

The Retford findings which have been quoted form a useful summary of some kinds of differences which are also revealed by the analysis of case study interview records and questionnaires. There are just a few exceptions of which four were striking. One of these was Rotary, where for various reasons not altogether within its control, the social motivation of members had apparently taken precedence over the overt public service objective. Another was a WEA branch whose members met perhaps mainly emotional needs by preserving painstakingly the trappings of study while avoiding its practice, and a third was the UIMWO, whose original objectives had been so largely replaced by substantial quantities of professional and contract work on behalf of the public sector that some few local clients but no local members could be found. The survival of the organisation and its useful professional activity appeared, on the surface at least, to have become the most noticeable objective, and it had ceased, to all intents and purposes, to be an LVO in the sense of our definition (cf. p. 4). A fourth organisation, the W London CA, was found to be unsuccessful in terms of its own objectives and as such mediated considerably less learning and change to its actual, while excluding the bulk of its potential membership. Even though it failed to meet its own objectives, it was successful as a landlord, and in that capacity this CA contributes to our findings through the experience of the organisations which it houses.

These four were the exceptions and, at little more than an eighth of the sample, they form an encouragingly low proportion. Among all the rest incongruence between organisational and member objectives and benefits was invariably beneficial. Our purpose here is to illustrate these matters generally, without trespassing on the detailed accounts to be given in subsequent chapters.

In all the remaining 27 case study organisations and, as far as could be judged, also in the Retford sample, the members shared the official objectives of the group and obtained those benefits which were intended. The degree to which this happened naturally varied among both organisations and individual members. But by and large it may be said that where the learning of a skill or subject, the practice of an activity or the pursuit of an interest was intended, or where simple sociability was desired, these things took place. Members who wanted to give service to and care for others, who wanted to publicise and propagate a point of view, or to engage in civic and developmental activity through organisations with these objectives, were able to do so.

This finding is important and satisfying in its own right. However, more important still is the discovery of the great range of learning, change and satisfaction over and above those which are deliberate, inherent in the organisation's objectives, and expected by their members. The one which was given priority almost universally, and reported as being of greater importance than the content objective of the organisation, is quite simply growth in confidence, and its ramifications and secondary effects of self-discovery, freedom in forging relationships and undertaking tasks, belief in oneself and in one's potential as a human being and an agent, and an ability to learn and change both in the context of the organisation's objectives *and* in others.

Almost invariably this is thought to derive from the mutual caring and support of the group as such, and the appreciation of the individual's contribution to it by fellow members. Reinforced by the sense of security arising from this, a substantial proportion of the respondents had taken on positions of responsibility within or outside the organisation, some of them for the first time in their lives. One hundred and ninety-seven members (36%) found themselves more effective in discharging responsibilities and 216 (39%) were serving as officers or committee members of their own LVO. Evidence from several case studies shows that other members, in addition to these, were discharging analogous responsibilities in other organisations. All of these had learned to undertake managerial and organising tasks and discovered a greater range of talent, energy and potential within themselves than they had previously suspected. Finally, 302 (55%) had learned, through these processes, to look at their own and the organisation's activities in the context of the social and political needs of their local community in itself and within a national context. Not a few had become active in some or all of these spheres. These are member responses, but observer evidence confirmed them.

We have deliberately used the geometric term "incongruence" in order to avoid value implications. However, it turns out to denote some characteristics which have a distinctly normative import:

- it has been shown to imply the addition of variable but always valuable learning and change *over and above what is expected*. In effect, an astonishing range and intensity of learning, attitudinal change and development is fermenting in most LVOs *in addition to* whatever is assumed to be their range of activities
- the result is a rapid and all too often ignored and wasted development of human potential. Rather than "unintended", this is *unpremeditated* learning, an uncovenanted access, a windfall as it were, of human capital arising from the voluntary sector. Society has yet to take proper cognisance of, and learn to invest it productively.

Unpremeditated learning and change grow in a variety of environments. In our experience the most marked examples include the two women's groups (NWR and WI), three outward-looking community-wide organisations (Ingleton CA, the Arts Centre and the Settlement) and an inward-looking one (Fifty-Plus), and three very specialised ones (Singers, Railway Trust and Mountain Rescue). All of these are in the strongly incongruent group, though they differ widely in other respects. However, they share one characteristic. Therefore:

- organisations which mediate most unpremeditated learning also make the greatest demands upon the active commitment of their members, and vice versa.

They include organisations with and without staff, large and small, with and without their own accommodation, with and without external funding and even without any money at all. It begins to look as if the quantity and quality of learning and change that takes place in most LVOs is not *primarily* the product of objectives, organisation or resources. The key to an understanding of the reciprocal effects of members and their organisations, and the reflection of these effects in learning and change, may well prove to lie elsewhere. Later chapters will suggest it could be found in our study of the characteristics of members' personal relationships with each other, and those of any leadership (whether or not paid), in members' growing awareness of their own needs and potential, and the level of demands inherent in membership.

Deliberate and Unpremeditated Learning

Even the small group of distinctly less successful organisations mediated *some* learning, though not necessarily that which their primary objectives enshrined. All groups mediated at least some deliberate learning – i.e. that which the group's objectives promised and which may well have the function of providing the conscious reason for joining. Most were found to be at least moderately successful in this, and many very much more so. The significant finding, however, is that all, including even the four least successful groups, mediated at least some unpremeditated learning and change. Moreover, the responses indicate that in the case of the 11 organisations listed on p. 42 above (just over one-third of the total) this was very strong. In 16 it ranged from strong down to moderate, and there were only four weak instances.

A trawl of the interviews shows that the great majority of respondents attached a high value to these unpremeditated learnings and resulting personal change *after experiencing them*, and indicated that they considered them even more important than the deliberate learning content of their membership. The following numerical examples illustrate this:

Diagram 9: Unpremeditated learning gains

Members responding	N = 552	%
Had gained general (as well as specific) sense of achievement/competence	359	65
Gained in ability to deploy and transfer knowledge/skills	323	54
Had improved discussion skills	312	57
Benefited from deepened personal relationships	231	42
Generally increased confidence	446	81
Mentioned beneficial effects on their occupation	314	57
Mentioned greater political awareness (not always beyond the LVO)	269	49

Unpremeditated learning always ranged more widely than the original specific purpose, and very often gave rise to far-reaching and sometimes profound personal change. Many respondents were modest in their claims and anxious not to give the impression that they took their activities or their outcomes over-seriously. Intellectual effort especially tended to be played down, probably as a form of understatement and not from conviction. However, whenever they touched upon these more personal and searching outcomes, false modesty was abandoned and full weight given to the personal importance of what had occurred, and to its wider impact on individuals and on organisations.

This chapter has demonstrated that the incongruent incidence of deliberate and unpremeditated learning and change reported to us occurs in all our samples, is rarely slight and often very great. The difference between the deliberate and unpremeditated categories of learning is real and is clearly perceived by our respondents. For all of them the deliberate category includes the overt skill, knowledge and activity content in-

herent in the organisation's aims, such as playing badminton successfully, learning about church architecture, understanding and coping with
the effects of arthritis in oneself and in fellow-sufferers, effective playgroup management or successful community organisation. For all our respondents the unpremeditated outcomes are those which almost
invariably were unexpected or not explicitly looked for, which are personal to them, not easily formulated or defined. They are deep-seated,
and have their outcomes in changes of attitude (especially growth in confidence) and re-definition of personal roles rather than immediate and
particular knowledge or skill. The benefits are carried into relationships
and activities generally. All this indicates that the unpremeditated learning is more fundamental and more lasting because it directly causes
change and development of the person, and it is often so perceived. It
links with, or is probably identical to what is described as personal learning on pp. 78–84 below.

None of this should suggest that deliberate learning and its role in
LVOs are unimportant. The opposite is clearly true. However, deliberate
learning seems to have an important additional function. Very few indeed of our respondents gave the impression that in joining their organisation they had looked for or even envisaged the more deep-seated
learning and change which had subsequently occurred. Apart from the
important but initially less deep-seated social motivation (which sometimes included such intentions as to fill time, do something with a friend
or, negatively, to get away from a spouse), it is the organisation's overt
objective which principally attracts people into membership. It continues
to form a legitimate and satisfying reason for belonging and, *as such*, becomes the vehicle that carries individual members from initially more
superficial to more fundamental learning and change. It enables them to
travel to the point, or points, of discovery where a vision of previously
unsuspected needs and satisfactions becomes a reality because the needs
have been met and the satisfactions experienced.

There is further evidence for a necessary connection between the deliberate and unpremeditated categories of learning and change: respondents from those organisations which were most consistently successful
in mediating the learning and change inherent in their *overt* objectives,
also reported the greatest variety and depth of unpremeditated learning.
It is tempting to look for a parallel between this deep stratification of individual learning activity, and the kind of organisational learning which
will be addressed in Chapter 7. It is certainly true that, when the organisations were grouped into high, moderate and low categories according
to their overt effectiveness, the parallel assessments of unpremeditated
development turned out the same in almost every instance. Finally, it
seemed not unlikely that it was the unpremeditated gains, more particularly, which tended to be transmitted both within the membership and to
the organisation itself and beyond it. Much of this will form the subject
of detailed study of our evidence especially in the following chapter.

A few more summary points emerge:

- the area of incongruence between deliberate learning derived from an organisation's overt objectives, and unpremeditated learning and change, is evidence of the success of organisations and individuals in maximising their potential

- there is a close and presumably causal relationship between an organisation's success in mediating its deliberate and overt learning and change, and the members' additional and unpremeditated benefits

- unpremeditated learning and change are deep-seated, lasting and enriching. They affect self-image, personal roles and relationships, attitudes and behaviour.

Chapter 5

Individual Learning and Change

The title of this chapter embraces many meanings, events and concepts. In 1964 J.A. Simpson, then a Staff Inspector for non-vocational Further Education in the Department of Education and Science, devised a classification of formal and informal adult education which circulated widely:

1. *Personal education* in the use of leisure, providing confidence in a subject or a skill but also satisfying unformulated need for creative experience, enjoyment of performance, achievement, self-respect, or success.
2. *Social education*, experience of association and relationships in groups with common purposes, possible participation in the corporate life of the institution, and concern for the betterment of the community.
3. *General education*, education in values, enhancement of powers of appreciation, discrimination and judgement and enlarging the range of the individual's interest and knowledge.

In many respects this remains a helpful statement. We have made our own attempt to sub-divide the seamless robe of adult learning and change, into *Social and Group, Content, Occupational, Political, and Personal learning* because for our purposes Simpson's categories were too broad and eclectically inclusive. Nevertheless each of our five embraces activities and experiences which spill over into others. Nor are learning and change clearly distinguishable terms in our context. Wherever we have tried to make clear distinctions between them we found them slipping between our fingers, each turning into the other, being interchangeably cause and effect. We have therefore refrained from defining our categories or borrowing definitions for them. Instead we have chosen to allow our respondents' evidence to complete its own jigsaw picture of what is involved.

The "social and group" category is intended to capture social and interpersonal benefits and learning, both individual and those derived from membership of a group or organisation, and their effects. "Content learning" is that which relates directly to the knowledge, skill or activity content of the particular organisations whose members were being interviewed. "Occupational learning" is any learning and change resulting from membership in the organisation which affects the respondent's performance, standing or development in their own occupational area, whether paid or, in the case of housewives for instance, unpaid. The "political" category embraces all forms of learning and change which relate to the individual's understanding and responsible participation in group activity *at all levels* from the particular organisation to the local community and to national and international issues. We used the "personal" heading to pick out and enter whatever learning had occurred which seemed *to the respondents concerned* to have affected, or changed them *personally* in ways that seemed significant to them. If some of these statements sound similar to others made to us earlier by the same individual, more often than not under the social and group category, their import for that individual is nevertheless different at least in degree and sometimes in kind, because they are felt to relate to a deeper stratum of their personality. It is certainly more significant.

Social Learning and the Effect of the Group

We have shown in Chapter 4 that this is the category of learning and change which very often sprang first to our respondents' minds and tended to assume greater importance than others. People not only saw it as generally important, they described it from a range of their own experiences. Few examples can be given here and readers should seek further illustrations and understanding from the case studies.

Some respondents denied social motives and satisfactions. This was most common in team sports carried on by organisations using the W London CA. Elsewhere talk of such motives caused initial embarrassment. The denial of social motivation at Ujima may have been due to the breakdown of relationships in that organisation. Male members of the S Wales WEA Branch denied them altogether until the female minority pointed out that they were real, agreeable, and even respectable. Indeed, generally almost twice as many women as men laid claim to various forms of social learning. Mountain Rescue Members denied any social significance to their group in the present, but agreed that it had been important to them during the Team's formative stages. Yet all their evidence confirmed the continuing central importance of the team relationship with its mutual confidence and reciprocal reliance. It welded extremely disparate individualists into a unit where co-operation, and within it the ability to switch from leadership to obedience from one moment to the next, could be essential to survival. It is this quality of social learning that could enable just one of them – otherwise a self-declared isolate – to admit that 'the team is my bridge to reality'.

It may be that for some, and perhaps for many respondents, social learning in the context of their LVO, though valued, is limited and superficial. Pigeon Fanciers and also organisations such as the Residents seemed to suggest that occasional good fellowship and learning to rub along together at a superficial level are as far as it goes – and who would deny their value? What seems interesting is that groups whose members responded in this way are either male or male-dominated. This issue will, at least by implication, surface again in the discussion of various kinds of women's groups.

However, after cool responses have been taken into account, it remains true that social learning, both as a personal bonus and as social education, figures more frequently than any category other than content learning. Of all individual members interviewed 92% spoke of the experience of membership as broadening their range of social contact and most saw it as a personal bonus and a social education. 40% (among them many unemployed men and young mothers) said that it actually created the opportunity of social contact for them. It was important to them to have this opportunity supplied to them, to be given the chance of being active in an organisation or group, and (especially for women) that 'it got (them) out of the house'. Membership had increased people's confidence in 446 (81%) instances, sometimes from a low level. The proportion who described themselves as fundamentally shy because lacking in confidence was surprisingly high. Indeed, the condition seemed so common that, occasionally, one was tempted to wonder if it was imaginary and assumed by the respondent as an unconscious display of personal modesty. Whatever the truth of this, there can be no doubt that for a very large proportion of informants, membership of an LVO had been their introduction to a wider range of people from a variety of social, occupational and educational backgrounds. They saw this, and their growing experience of sharing interests and co-operating with different kinds of people as a distinct benefit. They found themselves joining more readily in conversations and expressing their opinions and feelings.

Mutual tolerance, accepting and being accepted, knowing and being known by, their fellow members were seen by many as a source of emotional and not just social satisfaction. Thus 28% referred to increased tolerance and ability to accept, 42% to deeper relationships and 31% to being more able to commit themselves. Moreover, 'knowing people means you want to do things for them' was seen as the frequent and natural reaction to this, and the presumable source of another central aspect, the sense of mutual support and caring which was found to be typical of a high proportion of the organisations and not just the self-help groups, where it is central. There were few LVOs in our sample which did not provide repeated evidence of such mutual caring, from lifts and shared transport to visiting and nursing the sick, and other forms of long-term support. One (Fifty-Plus) was found to be performing all the functions of what would, elsewhere, be several different specialist self-help groups. In some groups, as will be shown below, the process of mutual support may extend to embrace members' families. All these aspects were regarded as sources, or results, of the enhanced personal and social confidence which respondents were experiencing.

Another function appeared repeatedly in connection with generalist groups, but also with two of the specialists: certain kinds of groups are a ready-made means for members, especially from elsewhere, to be integrated into a new community. This is worth illustrating from some of the LVOs where it was met. Thus members of the Playgroup, Wildlife, Kelvedon WEA and the Arts Centre reported how, on arrival in these places, joining the groups concerned had provided them not just with a friendly welcome but with a social network within which they could build a satisfying set of relationships as well as pursuing those activities which formed the organisation's objectives. In the case of the Settlement environmental factors made the organisation not just a welcoming network but a safe haven in a distinctly hostile environment, while at Ingleton CA there was evidence that an unknown but significant number of people actually moved to the village in order to reap the benefits of belonging. The WI and NWR groups had specific arrangements to recruit individuals on removal to their area and the NWR group had prepared a dossier of information about local services and institutions for their use.

The great majority of respondents (81%) gave evidence of the growth of personal confidence due to these and similar social learning experiences, the sense of 'being able simply to be' within the group, 'not having to wear a face', and the sense of liberation, energy and ability to take on learning tasks and responsibilities that resulted. It seemed significant that in a group like the NWR it was accepted as normal that this would carry some members into new networks and even new occupations, enabling some to 'grow out at the top of the group' as new ones came in. In smaller populations such as Sibsey's and Ingleton's the same phenomenon expressed itself less in the form of departure than of the accretion of more and wider responsibilities first within the organisation and later the local community. The particularly strong local networks observed there are likely outcomes.

A rather smaller group of organisations illustrated ways in which social learning and the confidence engendered by mutual support within the group act as essential stimuli to other kinds of learning. They are particularly valuable in helping to create the ambience and skill of a group, just as skill and ambience help to foster the personal relationships on which they thrive: the reciprocities retreat into the distance like endless mirror images of mutual learning and development. Particular evidence for such mutuality came from the Gardeners and the Railway Trust, and in more articulate terms especially from the Singers.

This fiercely specialist group consists almost entirely of people who have so little leisure that the group absorbs most or all of it and becomes the centre of their social lives. Yet normally social time consists of some 10 minutes of tea, biscuits and chat at the end of a concentrated evening rehearsal once a week. Nevertheless the social and group effects which members claim include everything which has been reported under this heading so far, and more: there is 'a closeness when we're there' and 'we know each other well enough to ring up and ask for anything'; 'there's a lot of caring when anyone's in trouble' and the potential tensions between very strong personalities are absorbed.

There seem to be several reasons for this. In the first instance the choir started "from the bottom up", and remains a group of friends who decided to sing together, rehearsing in each others' homes and appointing their own conductor. Secondly, the base in members' homes means that they 'allow each other closer to themselves' and involve families. This is reinforced by joint travel and residence at distant engagements, with families included. The outcome of these complex relationships is a dense network rather than a circle, and this can bear the strains and potential conflicts which arise under the stress of unusually high levels of demand made upon the time, effort and mutual tolerance of members.

The Writers and the Pigeon Fanciers provide partial and somewhat unusual parallels. In both, group meetings appear to be faintly reminiscent of tribal ritual before and after battle, first "firing up" members like a war dance for the critical effort, and afterwards enabling them to assimilate the experience in a wake. Apart from the institutionalised competition in these two groups there was surprisingly little competitive feeling to be found anywhere else in our sample. On the contrary, we were often told of the personal growth and 'satisfaction in *working with* others' as opposed to being isolated and limited by having to compete in working life. More generally, members in employment spoke of their voluntary activities as a welcome way of 'winding down', of relieving stresses at work. They enjoyed meeting fellow members, sharing experiences with them, and frequently discussing other topics, personal, local and national.

Special Categories of People

A sense of narrowing or limitation, as well as insecurity, is felt most strongly by those who are permanently or temporarily the victims of conditions or characteristics which distinguish them from what are, or seem to be, majorities. That sense is counter-balanced by feelings of not being unique, of belonging, and of mutual responsibility and assistance. Evidence emerged of these and other ways in which a sense of personal worth can be rebuilt and used to launch confident attempts to cope with particular persons' disadvantages and meet their needs. It emerges with special force among members of groups such as Aekta SH, whose members are doubly isolated by role and ethnicity, but as an organisation it is typical of self-help groups in general.

In a different way half the human race is disadvantaged. Three of our case study organisations (the NWR and WI Groups and the Widows' SH) are women's groups by definition. A fourth, the Playgroup, is so in practice. Whatever the objectives of these groups, the fact that they serve women gives them a special significance for their members although its precise nature may change with women's roles. One fact, however, does not change: 'Women need women' and belonging to something which is especially for them therefore has a particular value. 'There are a lot of things that women like to do with women.' Most felt that they are able to be 'more frank' in the absence of men. In women's groups 'Women can be in charge', 'they blossom, aren't edged out by men'. This was considered especially important for non-professional women, who 'wouldn't rise if men were around'. Women on their own were considered 'more supportive' of each other, 'interested and caring', and observers as well as members noted the freedom from competition in their groups.

There was also a distinct absence of any sense of ritualistic structure or behaviour, and of hierarchy, in all-woman groups. On the contrary, responsibility tended to be particularly widely dispersed, to the extent where, in the WI Group, every member who wanted or could be persuaded to take on any responsibility had one created for her if necessary. Almost each one wore an official hat, and many had responsibilities in other LVOs in addition. But the ambience was never starchy; efficiency was achieved with a great deal of informality and 'sheer fun'. It could be significant that when husbands of NWR group members tried to establish an informal discussion group of their own the attempt foundered.

Important as they were in general, these characteristics of women-only groups were seen to be most significant at periods of major role change. Some examples of such social learning support by the group at these times drew on the period of isolation experienced by so many women when they have young families. Group support was enabling them to cope, to maintain a sense of identity, proportion and of wider horizons. At the stage of emergence from exclusive domesticity, and then suffering from the almost universal loss of confidence in facing the 'outside' world and its tasks, women's groups were reported to be of special value, as they were again when supporting individuals preparing for a new or resumed career and making the requisite changes. All these factors apply *a fortiori* to a group such as the Widows' SH, where the role change is extreme and often destructive.

There is concomitant evidence from three of these groups that women's membership in their own groups can contribute powerfully to the social education of their menfolk. This will be discussed under the heading of transmission of learning.

Only one of our sample groups (Fifty-Plus) was specifically for elderly people but several others had objectives or characteristics which meant that they catered for a mainly elderly membership. They included organisations as varied as an adult education centre and a WEA branch (Guildhouse and S Wales WEA); self-help groups for arthritics and macular disease sufferers and the allotment holders.

All these provide powerful elements of social education within the group, but Fifty-Plus pays special attention to the value of this element and sets out deliberately to provide it by using other activities as vehicles of social learning. Thus its rambling group is not just seen as a source of interest and physical fitness; a rambling group also offers particularly varied social experience because of the way in which walkers spread out in smaller sub-groups. In consequence this activity was found to be especially valuable to new members and to the recently bereaved. Learning to swim in old age requires and elicits the extremely strong mutual support which has also been described in the case of the Singers, and builds confidence in proportion. The effectiveness of such group support and learning in helping old people to maintain a sense of secure identity and with it a constructive role in the community, an ability to learn, and personal health and independence, was repeatedly confirmed by independent evidence from medical and social services personnel.

The Railway Trust and Fifty-Plus were the only examples we happened to meet of groups making deliberate use of regular internal newsletters to enhance and celebrate people's sense of belonging to the LVO, and to keep sub-groups informed about each other's activities. In such large and heterogeneous organisations with many and diverse sub-groups this was likely to be especially appropriate.

Group Learning and Structures

The importance of group learning and mutual support within groups to the social education of their members has been variously illustrated. The way in which a network, rather than just an assemblage of separate relationships, affects this can be parallelled on a larger scale. Successful multi-purpose organisations (e.g. Ingleton CA, the Arts Centre, Bassetlaw CVS, Fifty-Plus, and possibly the Settlement) develop network structures which are strongly dynamic. In consequence they stretch far beyond themselves and embrace a wide variety of formally quite separate groups and activities.

This had also been true of the Guildhouse in its more dynamic past, when it hatched a number of major civic organisations which are now quite separate. However, in the other groups which have been referred to, the otherwise separate groupings came to overlap and support each other's concerns and activities. What had begun as the social education of individuals and their activities had become the social education of groups and communities. This may be contrasted with the W London CA whose proper objectives would have been analogous to those of the other five, but which had opted to abandon them. The result was that we found activities within this centre working in isolation from each other and the Association itself isolated not just from all the cognate organisations in its area but excluding the local community it was intended to serve.

Variations and their Causes

The very much higher incidence of social learning claimed by women has been mentioned. Other personal characteristics such as age, TEA or occupational background seemed to make no significant differences to social learning. On the other hand several characteristics of the organisations did. Taking organisational objectives first, the absolute number of those claiming social learning as a result of membership was high throughout, but especially so among women's organisations and physical activities, and less for those devoted to personal interests and advocacy. Learning to accept personal commitment was most pronounced in medium-sized groups (30–100 members), and these and large ones were better at creating social contact than the smaller. The number of groups with small, medium and large numbers of staff and similar gradations of external funding were insufficient for reliable conclusions to be drawn about the effects.

Content Learning

At the beginning of this chapter we admitted the project's difficulties in making absolute distinctions between different kinds of learning, between learning and change, and even between cause and effect where these can, and all too often do, turn into each other without waiting for the researcher's back to be turned. Confidence, perhaps the key word of the preceding section, acquired as a result of social learning and mutual support, enables content learning to proceed with enhanced chances of a successful outcome: 542 members (98%) made this point. Successful content learning – competence regardless of subject or skill – breeds confidence and all its individual, social and activity-related outcomes. The web of reciprocities is endless, but pattern is necessary to an intelligible account. The evidence will therefore be grouped under specific content, the extension of content, and additional skills and attitudes related to the two preceding aspects of the learning process. Each of these groups will spawn its own sub-sections.

Specific Content

This is, of course, the most obvious kind of learning to be observed in LVOs, and requires little argument and illustration. Some distinctions may, however, be introduced.

In generalist organisations a variety of different content areas are available. The most obvious instance is the wide-ranging programme of academic and arts subjects offered by an adult education centre such as the Guildhouse. Fifty-Plus offers a different balance, with a prevalence of physical education and skills and a more deliberate social education content. Ingleton CA adds social activities, social and economic development, and advocacy and representation to these others. The Arts Centre, Wildlife and the Settlement, although focused, respectively, upon the arts, environmental studies, and basic education, social and community development, nevertheless offer a range of mutually nourishing choices.

Specialist organisations are those which focus on one particular activity or concern, though they are not necessarily confined in their interests and sympathies. The greatest potential for variety within a specialism exists in the Railway Trust. Its specialism is real and the members pursue it with passion. However, it is so wide that members must between them find or create subsidiary specialist expertise in areas as far apart as catering and coach painting, management accountancy and signalling, track laying, engine driving, and many more. Moreover, the organisation requires a considerable degree of mutual information and understanding of the various disciplines to achieve its high degree of efficiency.

Other specialist activities are as it were inherently multi-disciplinary. Pigeon Fanciers cannot specialise within their pursuit because all have to acquire expertise ranging from genetics to meteorology in addition to that required in caring for their birds and managing the complexities of feeding and finance. Allotment gardeners proved no less varied in their lore. Archaeology involves skills of observation, surveying, excavation, finds processing and report writing in addition to study of the subject as such. Members of the Mountain Rescue team have to be expert in all forms of mountaineering, first aid, search and rescue, and radio communications, but also in the skills of coping with trauma, of teaching safe enjoyment of the mountains and answering questions about the environment. It is only among the most specialised self-help groups such as the one serving sufferers from macular disease or a carers' group such as Aekta that specialisation becomes as focused as it is also among the Writers and the Singers.

The Extension of Content

Wherever a subject or activity is being pursued with dedication people soon become aware of its multiple links with others. These open up the possibility of a general education built around the chosen centre by means of centrifugal forays or expanding circles. There is also the ever-present possibility of infection. Thus, at the Arts Centre there was repeated testimony to the effect of theatre stewarding upon personal taste and practice, and the role of exhibitions in the foyer in awakening hitherto unconscious interests and talents. Proximity to other activities or hearing about them in the common room or at some function was said to be the stimulus that led many respondents at the Guildhouse, at Ingleton CA and in Fifty-Plus to take up new interests.

Extension proper is different from this and a few examples will illustrate it. It involves processes such as wild flower or bird enthusiasts joining the Wildlife Trust and becoming aware of the way particular forms of flora and fauna depend on a whole nexus of environmental factors. It appears in the practice of some allotment holders who conduct what amounts to scientific experiments and record their findings, of playgroup members developing an interest in the study of child psychology, members of the Fifty-Plus group moving from swimming and badminton for fun and gentle exercise to systematic coaching, ramblers making a study of ancient buildings, Residents becoming aware of housing law and the Singers becoming interested in international affairs as a result of their contacts and performances.

Additional Skills and Attitudes

Members of LVOs thus acquire substantial knowledge or skills in the process of pursuing whatever may be the objectives of their organisation or activity, at least as it is interpreted by themselves. It might be as apparently simple as producing tea and biscuits for an old people's club – which requires catering skills about quantities and time and costs – or need an umpire's mature understanding of the laws of cricket. The point just made about trauma not only in the victims of mountaineering accidents but their companions and the rescuers themselves illustrates the learning of skills and attitudes not directly connected with a subject nor part of its formal or informal content.

At the *personal level* these include attitudes such as sensitivity and maturity in the giving and receiving of criticism, as in the Writers' Workshop, or the moral and physical courage required of staff and volunteers at the Settlement, the integrity of the honest broker in Bassetlaw CVS between local government and the LVOs, the supportive generosity of WI and NWR group members, the tough persistence of Pigeon Fanciers and the self-control and devoted stamina of the Singers.

The *interpersonal level*, too, requires attitude change, and 46% of members claimed it had taken place. They spoke of learning to be tolerant, patient, energetic when necessary in their relationships with each other and with non-members. People had learned how to approach and negotiate with others, including officials. Volunteer drivers had learned how to be patient, tolerant, but not allow themselves to be imposed upon by excessive demands. Residents' Association members had learned how to handle themselves in their exposed position between local government and local people. Diplomacy in getting the best out of prima donnas and shrinking violets, in making people and organisations aware of their own gaps and weaknesses without destroying a relationship, and encouraging them to constructive endeavour – all these skills and qualities and attitudes were represented by the evidence which has been collected, and shown to be organically linked to other learning processes in the activity of the LVOs.

Learning at the two former levels was expected. What was not expected was the surprising amount and quality of effective learning (and not uncommonly informal teaching) of *organising, managerial and civic skills and attitudes:* 42% of the sample spoke of this. Moreover, 36% had learned or improved their ability to discharge responsibility, 43% had learned to co-operate with others, and these changes must have borne some relationship to the general improvement in interpersonal (46%) and discussion skills (57%).

What needs to be borne in mind first of all is that an LVO is voluntary, and has a structure. Almost invariably the organisations we met had an elected committee and elected officers: people had learned and were continually re-learning the skills and attitudes of democratic government. At the time when the case studies were conducted 39% of members were serving on their organisations' committees. This total excludes those who had served in the past, and it also excludes such responsibilities borne elsewhere. The questionnaire data base adds all forms of internal and external responsibility and shows that 66% of LVO members (65% of women and 67% of men) carry some form of elected responsibility. As new individuals were elected they had to learn not just organising, managerial and financial skills but the attitudes which enable officers of democratic organisations to conduct their business constructively and relate to staff where these are employed. Whether because they had some form of financial link with local government or because people saw them as their representatives, they also had to acquire skills and attitudes appropriate to citizens who represent others and need to influence government, at whatever level, on behalf of their organisation.

It was this range of learning which enabled the Guildhouse, alone among such centres in Britain, to survive under lay leadership when it lost the grant that paid its warden. It must be the reason why the evidence shows WEA members at Kelvedon to be disproportionately prominent in local offices and responsibilities, why outside observers found that the WI group provides the great majority of that small circle of people who bore the senior responsibility for village activities and affairs. It was this kind of learning, too, which underlies the exceptional level of managerial, planning and political capacity which was independently attested at Ingleton CA. On the other hand, throwing excessive amounts of money at an organisation (Ujima) which lacked the managerial skills and the structure, without providing the necessary training, was to invite disaster.

Who Learns? Generalities and Important Exceptions

Ever since Trenaman (1957) it has been known that there is a causal link between the duration of people's initial or first cycle education measured in terms of TEA, and the readiness of these same people, when adult, to participate in formal or informal educational and cultural or other demanding leisure pursuits: the greater the age to which their first cycle education has extended, the greater is the likelihood that they will later be broadly culturally active; the less that age, the less the likelihood. Trenaman's original work has been endlessly replicated, almost invariably without acknowledgment and without significant development. The effect he identified is therefore appropriately named after him.

The participation issue has often been confused by linking it to occupation, which in turn is used to determine social class. But occupation depends patently upon TEA in the great majority of individuals, and it is therefore initial educational experience which is the significant root factor. This argument admittedly ignores the degree to which class attitudes starve that root in a system which offers equality of opportunity while denying the opportunity of equality.

Wherever possible TEA was collected during interviews, and in the questionnaire survey it was a standard item. The minimum figures include those who left school at whichever was the lowest permissible age when they reached it, i.e. 14, 15 or 16 according to their ages. The overall statistics for the case study members are as follows:

Diagram 10: TEA of case study respondents (N=522)

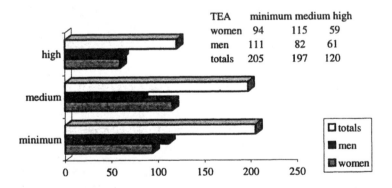

TEA	minimum	medium	high
women	94	115	59
men	111	82	61
totals	205	197	120

The main and secondary data bases confirm from these and other figures that the Trenaman effect operates almost as strongly in the LVOs as it does in course-based adult education. Comparison is difficult because the last reasonably confidence-inspiring statistics relating TEA to adult education class membership date from the period before systematic fee increases at many times the rate of inflation banished from adult education those who are neither affluent nor conspicuously deprived.

Comparison must therefore be based on field experience more than imperfect statistics. It suggests strongly that, when compared with adult education classes during the 1960s and early 1970s, when the proportion of students with low TEAs was growing steadily, LVOs today show a not entirely dissimilar picture. There are certain kinds of activity such as allotment gardening and pigeon fancying which are (and always have been) mainly the preserve of people with low TEAs and subsequent lower category employment. Thus 35 of 40 Gardeners and 19 of 20 Pigeon Fanciers interviewed had received whatever was the minimal first cycle education in their youth.

LVOs concerned with the arts, academic study and general education tended to attract mostly people with medium and some high TEAs, but also a significantly higher proportion of people with a low TEA than would normally have been expected. Using the figures from the main data base, the NWR Group, Ingleton CA, Fifty-Plus and Writers drew over 25% and up to 33%, and the WI Group as many as 61% of these. The 75% and 59% at the S Wales WEA branch and the Settlement were due to their special circumstances. Among the questionnaire respondents as many as 16% of the minimum TEA group had subsequently improved their qualifications and their livelihood by means of mature study. However, this sample is unrepresentative and the proportion untypical, as was explained above (p. 11).

There have always been such exceptions to the Trenaman effect, individuals who were not held back by limited initial educational experience, and who were to be found in formal adult education, in mature study, and in LVOs otherwise consisting of medium- and high-TEA personnel. No systematic research is known to us which has investigated what stimulates these individuals to cross barriers. We have not conducted such research ourselves. Yet if this gap in our knowledge could be filled, both the education system and voluntary organisations would become aware of ways in which the limiting aspects of the Trenaman effect could be neutralised and more opportunities of equality created.

It may therefore be significant that our case studies revealed the presence of strikingly high proportions of low TEA individuals in certain organisations where they are statistically unexpected, as well as in traditionally working-class organisations. If we can identify what distinguishes these from others where such individuals are not to be found, then one or more causes will be revealed and with them perhaps some means of serving the educationally underprivileged more effectively.

The presence of high proportions of low-TEA individuals in *some* intellectually and otherwise than mainly physically (such as football or boxing) demanding organisations is traditional, and respondents' evidence shows that many or most were following in the footsteps of fathers or other influential elders. This pattern differs substantially from another, namely the presence of a higher than expected proportion (26% of respondents including a disproportionate number of volunteer tutors) of low-TEA individuals of either sex in Fifty-Plus and a majority of them (61% of respondents) in the WI Group. In both organisations these originally low-TEA members took part in a wide variety of activities. At Sibsey, moreover, it was clear that they were no less likely than those with medium and high TEAs to involve themselves in intellectually and aesthetically demanding activities, in taking on responsibilities, and in general active citizenship. There could, therefore, be certain features or conditions in both of these organisations which run counter to the Trenaman effect. At Sibsey these appear so strong as to nullify it altogether.

What are the special characteristics of these four organisations, and are any of them common to all? Gardeners, Pigeon Fanciers, Fifty-Plus and the WI Group are all highly intensive and involving, inherently so in the case of the first two and through their social and educational momentum in the second pair. Fifty-Plus also includes an unknown but possibly noticeable element of medical and social referrals, but this may be discounted as a causative factor because unconnected with TEA.

Respondents from Fifty-Plus and the WI Group were outstandingly articulate about social learning, social education, group coherence and mutual caring as deliberately fostered and strongly maintained characteristics of their organisations' activity. Thus all WI members spoke of mutual support and all Fifty-Plus members made emphatic references to it; all WI members gave the value of social contact as the motive for joining and 24 out of 27 among Fifty-Plus agreed. Members of the WI and of Fifty-Plus showed themselves to be more conscious of these motives and benefits than the Gardeners (31 of 40) and far more than the Pigeon Fanciers (no mentions) as a source of their confidence and energy in undertaking activities and responsibilities which they felt they could not otherwise have faced. Enjoyment of superficial levels of social contact was, of course, an obvious factor for Gardeners and occasionally for some Pigeon Fanciers, and there were mentions of mutual practical assistance, especially from allotment holders. However, the differences were not only numerical; the descriptive content of the responses shows that there were distinct qualitative differences between, on the one hand, the experience of a deep mutuality in the WI Group and to a lesser but comparable extent in Fifty-Plus, and, on the other, the pleasant sociability and occasional assistance among gardeners and the rather lesser version of this among Pigeon Fanciers.

The attributes found at Sibsey WI and Fifty-Plus, together with much informality and a kind of highly developed capacity for enjoyment, showed up more strongly in the responses from these two organisations than in any others in our sample. Are there important clues here? Should we perhaps begin to think in terms of a constructively developmental "Sibsey effect", based on the deliberate and special quality of *relationships* and the provision of opportunities for *specific involvement*, as a counter to the Trenaman effect's limitations on the educationally underprivileged?

Another factor which is likely to help individuals with minimal educational experience cross the barrier was determined statistically. If the total sample of member respondents is broken down into minimum, medium and high TEA groups and cross-tabulated with the high and low incongruence categories (as defined in Chapter 4), the following information emerges:

Diagram 11: Case study respondents – TEA and incongruence (N=522)

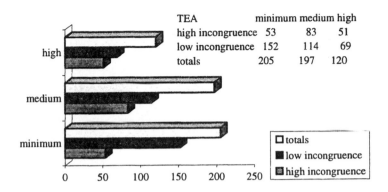

TEA	minimum	medium	high
high incongruence	53	83	51
low incongruence	152	114	69
totals	205	197	120

□ totals
■ low incongruence
▨ high incongruence

This shows that individuals with minimum TEA are most likely to breach the barrier via activities where there is a relatively low degree of incongruence between organisational objectives and personal intentions and outcomes. Typically, these are specialist activities. The prime example (the WI Group) is strongly incongruent and the two findings thus *seem* to run counter to each other. However, both sets of statistics are highly significant. Since both findings are evidently true, both describe ways across the barrier.

There are a number of ways in which the general findings about content learning become more varied when they are considered in relation to particular personal and organisational characteristics. Oddly enough there was only one respect in which women and men differed: a highly significant (in both senses) majority of men claimed to have learned much about the practice of co-operation. Age was not significant, but the Trenaman effect showed up clearly in relation to TEA and the process of learning to shoulder and discharge responsibility: the response was high for all three groups but the medium TEA group (47%) was nearly twice as high as the minimum group (26%), with the 20-plus group in between at 40%.

It was interesting to find that funding and staffing had no significant statistical effects on content learning. There are no surprises where straight content learning in relation to main organisational objectives is concerned. As soon as more general content-related learning such as organising skills and discharging responsibility are considered, differences emerge. Straight content skills improve most where the personal objectives are sport, practical activities, the arts and service. Organising skills and the discharge of responsibility are highest in women's groups, physical and social activities, and higher in generalist activities rather than specialist ones.

Learning and Occupations

Generally speaking the incidence of occupationally-related learning is equal between the sexes, except that reverse benefits from work to the LVO are more common among men. Age is not significant, but there are interesting differences due to TEA. Skill or content learning, acquired in the LVO and benefiting occupation, rise in parallel with TEA – another echo of the Trenaman effect. In contrast to this the process of learning in the LVO the skills which allow work to be planned and organised more efficiently is especially significant among respondents with minimum TEA.

A substantial minority (180) of responses produced no evidence either way of any relationship between the personal effects of their LVO membership and their occupations. This does not mean that there were none, and the interview sometimes first revealed the existence of such effects to the respondents as well as the interviewer. However, 58 specifically stated that there was no connection, and their membership of an LVO was deliberately separate, a recreation in the literal sense of the word, whose boundaries they defended staunchly against what they regarded as defilement by everyday pursuits: a Singer had insisted on flying home from a business trip abroad to attend the weekly rehearsal. An even more numerous group consisted of housewives who told us they had learned to rationalise and organise that occupation to stop it interfering with their LVO activity. Husbands who had learned to take on household duties on a regular basis in support of their wives' LVO activities were much less numerous.

However, 57% of member respondents mentioned some kind of occupational effect. Of these 131 were women and 183 men. We subdivided occupational learning into four subsidiary aspects: learning which is directly applicable to occupational tasks; generic skills and attitudes which influence performance at work; skills, attitudes and attributes learned in membership of an LVO which influence the way members are perceived at work; and those which contribute in some way to the performance of other individuals there.

Directly Applied Learning

Evidence under this heading covered a surprisingly wide range. One hundred and twenty-five respondents (23%) gave examples of skills or knowledge acquired in an LVO being applied in their daily work and there were 15% of instances where the process operated in reverse. Occasionally there was a direct cross-over as in the case of members of an LVO such as the Wildlife Trust who were acquiring knowledge of direct use to the conservation jobs for which they were training or which they occupied. Organisations such as Bassetlaw CVS, the Settlement, UIMWO, the Guildhouse, the Kelvedon WEA and NWR Groups, were providing opportunities for mature study and emotional support for members engaged in that demanding discipline as well as subsequently, when setting out on new careers. The Settlement ran a sound and original training scheme for mainly young adults with learning difficulties.

All these LVOs were thus enabling an encouraging number of previously unqualified adults to enter the labour market. Ujima had provided careers advice and encouragement. One of the Writers had
obtained a post in arts administration, class tutors were improving their
skills and using them elsewhere, school teachers were learning what it is
like to be a pupil, and taking the lesson back to their schools, Rotarians
were widening their business understanding and picking up useful contacts, office and stage technician volunteers received training which led
to jobs. Only students in adult education classes (for instance upholstery
at the W London CA and a variety of more intellectual subjects elsewhere) took their interest to the point of formal qualification enabling
them to teach or practise it for gain.

Generic Skills and Attitudes

We have no evidence that membership of a Women's Institute, or even
pigeon racing, necessarily turns people into better aircraft fitters or ex-
port salesmen. However, there is overwhelming evidence that especially
the generic skills and attitudes which are most valued by respondents
are also directly transferable to and valued in their occupations. Competence, confidence, interpersonal and organising skills and readiness to
take on and discharge responsibility make people better at almost any
job. They also alter the persona they present to other people; they become more impressive as well as more effective. Respondents (29% of
them) gave numerous examples of such skills and attitudes which had
eased or indeed enhanced their performance at work, but the key word
which was mentioned almost invariably was confidence: it was the confidence acquired through membership of the LVO which had enabled the
skills and attitudes to develop, or to be deployed. Responsibility with the
LVO invariably meant planning, organising, ability to discuss and to listen, to tolerate disagreement and to stand up for one's own point of
view. More generic skills learned in organisations were systematic policy-making and long-term planning and organisation, which some Pigeon Fanciers took across to their work, and the study skills which took a
number of women in particular into resumed study, and qualification for
new careers.

Members of self-help groups learned skills such as systematic organising which prepared them for the problems they were going to face
when, for instance, eyesight deteriorated further. Perhaps the commonest experience under this heading was that of people who had learned
organising, managerial and negotiating skills as officers and members of
committees and who took them from the LVO to all forms of paid work
and to elected office.

Maintenance of the habit of learning and improvement of learning
skills do not depend on subject. Many, including one chartered engineer,
had acquired writing skills in LVOs which opened the way to responsibility and promotion at work, as did study skills, mastered in archaeology, for a banker. Learning to express oneself in discussion and to
develop public speaking skills had led to local government or union office and to managerial positions. Sixteen per cent gave specific examples

of the application to tasks at work of having learned to be more systematic, and to plan. Almost every school teacher we interviewed told us that membership of their LVO had first given them the confidence to forge easy relationships with adults in general, and parents and governing body members in particular. In addition they had been able to enhance their teaching by means of knowledge and skills gained in the LVO.

Some unusual but productive relationships between LVO and work were found at the Railway Trust. Here a retired museum curator was functioning as an honorary curator, a volunteer signaller was developing self-study texts for signallers in general. Volunteer coach painters were contracted back by the Railway Trust to the employer who had made them redundant, but found that this and other skills were still required on an occasional basis and could only be found in the LVO. Finally a personal testimony to the effect of a voluntary centre at its best: a Guildhouse member had joined at an early age and had 'absorbed my personal standards from the example of (the warden)'. That led to continued study and responsibility in the centre, and then to a responsible job. When she married and started a family she applied what she had learned to her home, added child psychology to her studies, got interested in education, and trained as a teacher. Like many other women respondents she had, on the way, learned to value herself, had ceased being afraid to hold and proclaim her own opinions, and become a 'self-educator'.

Skills, Attitudes and Personal Attributes which Influence Standing at Work

Learning to value and assert themselves in their own right had influenced the way in which many women respondents were perceived at work, and the 'surge of (justified) confidence' which most members had experienced also had this effect: 84 of them gave instances of it. There were also more specific links, some simple and some complex and potentially important. A salesman known to be active in a worthy cause felt that he was being trusted as a friend when he called on business customers. Independent evidence confirmed that responsible office in recognised voluntary organisations raised the status of some individuals, such as teachers, among their colleagues.

The experience of responsibility, wherever it is held, does something to the personality which is carried into every compartment of life. However much the members of the Mountain Rescue denied it, external observers were unanimous in mentioning their raised status at work as well as in the local community, simply because it was their heightened capacities and skills to which people turned in crises. Archaeology seems to have little direct carry-over to the world of ordinary jobs, but the cachet of unusual expertise clings, and leads to the occasional assumption that whatever is unexpected or problematic may be safely passed to amateur archaeologists in a council office for solution. One assumes that in so far as they have learned to gather and analyse evidence and solve the problems it presents, their colleagues could do worse.

Contributions to the Performance of Others

Our respondents produced little direct evidence of this, though rather more came from some of the observers. It was claimed that volunteer experience of management and organisation was passed on particularly often and was usually accepted with alacrity as being practical and having been acquired in demanding circumstances. The behaviour of a school teacher who had held a laborious honorary office in a large organisation had initially surprised her colleagues. It struck them as a form of wilful martyrdom but eventually won their respect and, in some instances, co-operation. It may well be that learning and change undergone in LVOs are more often influential through the modest, unconsciously given and absorbed example of enthusiasm and dedication than in any other way, but it is in its nature that it would leave no evidence.

A special case: there remains the peculiarly fascinating experience of the Settlement (the Bede House Association) with its close interlocking of voluntary work, training and paid occupation within a single LVO. It is best described by an extract from Case Study 17 in Vol. 3, pp. 38ff. of our fieldwork publications:

> *The principles of settlement work, financial exigencies and personal skill among paid staff have jointly created a pattern of 'employment' and of relationships between paid and voluntary workers which are unique among the case studies carried out by our team. ... a continual two-way flow and therefore a sense of equality between volunteering and paid employment, or sometimes a co-existence of both within the same person.*
>
> *People volunteer for a wide variety of tasks, are cherished and trained. If they show exceptional potential they may be offered short-term paid part-time work and immediate training. A few fail at this stage, and their services have to be diverted or dispensed with, but selection appears to be made with skill and is usually successful. If there is money, or a newly financed project, a part-time paid ex-volunteer might graduate to full-time work. Several full-time staff specifically stated that it is Settlement policy, wherever possible, to start out by filling part-time posts with volunteers who have proved both their ability and dedication and their readiness to go on learning. Recruitment is, of course, open, but the experience and training of volunteers seem, reasonably, to favour their chances. The system has proved itself not just in the quality of teaching and other tasks performed, but in what it does to develop the potential of volunteers, and in improving the area's meagre leadership resources. 'Volunteers get an enormous amount out of it ... you can encourage them to do things they wouldn't dare do on their own, or aren't ready for unless you support them. They progress very rapidly.'*
>
> *On the other hand money all too commonly runs out, a project*

ceases, and so, consequently, does paid work. But not so employment: it seems to be taken for granted that one may, and does, switch from paid employment to voluntary work just as easily as from volunteering to paid employment. It is not unusual for an individual to be paid for part-time work and to be working voluntarily at the same time at either the same or another task. Nothing that could be described as a firmly uni-directional career path exists here. Most full-time and contract staff, and all part-timers and volunteers, find themselves on a kind of Jacob's ladder, moving between roles, and it is a single ladder, not two separate ones.

This pattern shows signs of becoming more common among LVOs in the social and welfare field, because core funding is disappearing and ad hoc funding uncertain and short term, or obtained from some TECs as time-limited training placements for volunteers.

The extent of this inter-penetration is unique in our sample, but it seems unlikely that the pattern is unknown elsewhere. The blend of membership, volunteering, training (and qualification) at various levels, and paid work, seems especially appropriate to large organisations active in caring, developmental work and in environmental concerns. Apart from its relevance to the current topic of learning and employment, the passage is of great interest in the context of the relationship between paid and unpaid, lay and professional workers and the nature of leadership in LVOs. Some analogies were also found in the Railway Trust, and we shall return to these matters in Chapters 7 and 9.

Political Learning

It is, perhaps, appropriate to refer again to the very broad and inclusive sense in which the term is used here: "... all forms of learning and change which relate to understanding and responsible participation in group activity *at all levels* from the particular organisation to the local community and to national and international issues."

Both politicians and locally-based officials confirmed the high level of democratic activity which is indicated by member responses under this head. Altogether 76% thought they had become more aware of public policy issues, if sometimes only as they were experienced within the LVO concerned, where 73% made this claim. Rather less but still more than half at 59% said they had become more aware of broader social issues and 49% had become more aware politically as a result. 30% had become more aware of specific political implications at a local, national or supra-national level, and 25% had taken overt political action (speaking, writing, advocating).

None of this is new in principle. The link between responsibility and personal development was well documented in Wilcox (1952), a study of members of 10 community associations. The analogous link between actively demanding study (regardless of subject content) and readiness to shoulder and discharge responsibility is documented in Elsdon (1962), which concludes that 'in so far as any institution does not foster a student's sense of responsibility it is liable to stifle it'. A Report by HM Inspectors (Education and Science, 1973) addresses the subject and finds that it is the most committed students in the adult education centre under review who are also active in responsible positions as committee members and volunteers. At the time of the study 10% of the total student body were involved in responsible positions and the centre's management.

Accounts such as these draw their evidence from relatively confined territory, and our concern in this chapter is with all kinds of what we term political learning and activity in LVOs. Politics in that sense is rather like a Russian doll. It is substantial and large-featured where it is concerned with understanding and action upon major national and international themes. However, if it is unscrewed it turns out to conceal learning and action about all kinds of broad political, social and inter-group patterns. Inside this there is understanding and action about one's own group or organisation as such and in relation to others and the larger body politic. Within this again there are the initial processes of personal commitment to the organisation, taking responsibility within it and acquiring the skills and knowledge of organising and management, of analysis and negotiation, which go with involvement at that level but form the germ of what is needed at the others.

Like all similes this one is no more than suggestive. In practice, the four levels are more of a continuum, but they offer a structure which groups the evidence as follows:

- Responsibility, skill, knowledge and action:
  - within the LVO
  - on behalf of the LVO vis-à-vis others
  - within broader patterns
  - at national and international levels.

Responsibility, Skill, Knowledge and Action within the LVO

LVOs are mostly small and even the few which have large memberships, such as the Railway Trust, Fifty-Plus or the Guildhouse, devise substructures small enough to foster intimacy, a feeling of knowing and being known. This means that our respondents found they could grasp even these large organisations. They had a feeling of belonging ('I feel I *own* this community', as one said of the Settlement), of having a stake in it, and that something was owing from them to the organisation. They connected the origins of this with the confidence engendered by relationships within the group – what we have described as social learning – and with the more specific content learning and consequent joint action shared with fellow members.

Respondents commonly told us that when they originally joined their LVO they simply wanted to get on with learning or doing whatever it was about. Any interest or understanding they developed beyond this had developed later from the experience of membership. Thus a Rotarian had joined for the sake of the social life; it was the subsequent experience of being involved with others in service activities which had first made him aware of social needs and social problems, and stimulated his political interests.

Experience of the group and the personal development it triggered became the germs which grew into a variety of perceptions and skills. Respondents had learned to listen to other people, to discuss rather than debate or argue, to tolerate disagreement, to think it possible they might be mistaken. They also learned to develop opinions which were genuinely their own – like the WEA members whose current affairs class had 'cracked our prejudices' and surprised some of them into making voting decisions 'not inherited from our parents'. Moreover, people had learned to express their opinions and, where necessary, to stand up and defend them or even to advocate causes, as young members of the Settlement were regularly doing vis-à-vis local council committees and Derby Widows and others vis-à-vis various public services.

The confidence to think one's opinion worth holding and defending – in essence to value and properly assert oneself – figured strongly as a wholly appropriate aim not just of women-only organisations but also of some others which had special groups for women, or provided developmental and career change groups for them. The needs of women had yet to be acknowledged where, as in the Railway Trust, they formed a small minority of the membership and tended to be concentrated in the traditionally low status activity of catering. By contrast, men's occupations in this organisation offered a wide range of responsible tasks and offices.

Taking on specific responsibilities within an organisation could and was often found to be stressful. 'At times I found it quite frightening ... the actions and feelings that could be provoked ... sorting out personal and impersonal and being aware one really does represent others.' A number of organisations complained to us that it was difficult to find new and younger successors for long-term office holders and committee members. There is, of course, no way in which responsibility can be taught; it can only be learned through the process of experiencing it. But in organisations which had faced the need for turnover and deliberate succession we learned of practical and sensitive ways in which new office bearers were eased in and supported by more experienced members. Three of our sample organisations (the NWR and WI Groups and Mountain Rescue) had introduced a maximum period of tenure and experienced no difficulty in maintaining the policy. It may be significant that all three were working on the basis of a maximum dispersal of responsibility. For different reasons and in different ways each ensured that most or all members were given experience of bearing responsibility and learning to wield it.

If experience of responsibility was found to develop the skills of wielding it, it was responsibility, too, that was found to bring out people's latent talents and capacities, including the ability to lead others, which had so often surprised respondents in themselves. They had learned not only to belong and be committed, but to co-operate deliberately in the formation and fostering of a group and its aims, in finding the highest common denominator, setting targets, shaping policies, identifying interests and representing them.

We found a high proportion of respondents had, consciously or otherwise, received an effective training in the skills of democratic representation and management. Many had thought about them and articulated their thoughts for us. They included not just the high percentage (39%) currently serving but an unquantifiable addition to take account of turnover and of service in other organisations. This was the more important because these were also the individuals who linked organisations with wider networks outside, whether local or national: 'It gave me a real interest in politics as a whole which I'd never had before.'

Responsibility, Skill, Knowledge and Action on Behalf of the LVO

The transition from internal responsibility to work on the LVO's behalf, or to individual activity inspired by it, can occur in a variety of ways. In the case of the NWR group, talks given to them by members and an outsider had crystallised several concerns which were new to members and which were taken up by some, leading to developments in fields as various as a women's shelter and changes at local schools. The interests of various individuals at the Guildhouse had led to the formation of several important civic organisations; Widows' SH were running regular counselling sessions for all comers and the Railway Trust had formed an effectively symbiotic relationship with the local authority's leisure and tourist services. Wildlife Trust members individually and through the Trust were active in various environmental campaigns, Archaeologists were serving on their local authority's environmental protection committee, Writers were campaigning for almost anything and the Playgroup was gradually inserting itself into the management of the village hall and extending the committee's horizons.

Anyone in a self-help group has to learn not just how to organise but to be an advocate for their group's special needs, and, more often than not, to negotiate on behalf of the group with various services and with professionals who may have a poor opinion of lay people trying to paddle their own canoe. All the sample organisations needed the support of their members' advocacy, and the skill was learned by many and applied to a wide range of other issues as well.

Much more complex political learning and organisation are needed in tasks incumbent on members of larger organisations, and especially those which face financial problems. A community association such as Ingleton CA has to manage itself and its own provision but must also foster and where necessary control the large number of semi-independent daughter organisations. It has to represent them, and itself, to the local authority both as partial dependants on it, and as its partners in other respects. It has to manage staff paid by the authority, staff who are also independent of it in part of their duties. It has to represent the social and cultural aspirations of the local community to its administrative body, the parish council – and membership of the two ruling bodies is almost identical. No wonder there is within this organisation a strong awareness of politics, an understanding of the political significance of many of its activities, and a high level of administrative, organising and planning expertise has been built up over the years.

This had not happened in the other community association in our sample. Owing to the absence there of a responsible membership and dispersal of powers, all authority had become concentrated in the hands of paid staff backed by a group of directors who depend on that staff for the information on which they base their decisions. Here democratic life has to be looked for in a quite separate local community organisation which is for practical purposes excluded from the centre. A not dissimilar situation, except for the absence of independent local development, appeared to obtain in UIMWO.

At the Settlement the long tradition of training in democratic responsibility has been reinforced by the dire financial situation. Paid staff can negotiate, but the most telling representation is conducted by volunteers and indeed members of the various sub-groups from the youth club up. For this they have to learn to master briefs, to understand the place of their own and other voluntary organisations and the way they relate to the public services – and to present their case to local councillors who are used to deputations. No wonder here, as at Ingleton CA, a strong awareness of and interest in politics and especially public services issues pervades the membership.

Responsibility, Skill, Knowledge and Action within Broader Patterns

Perhaps the commonest and simplest way in which several sample organisations had moved beyond their internal or local preoccupations was in joining the national campaign to save adult education from the misfortunes brought upon it by recent legislation. The various major issues which are regularly addressed by the National Federation of Women's Institutes, including Sibsey, are another example. An LVO staff member who had recently come from work for a local education authority had had to learn 'how to cope with being on the inside of pressure. ... the nightmare of being the battleground between central and local government ... and at the mercy of local politics'. It meant he had to learn how to campaign for the survival of his organisation while building up the confidence and the knowledge of his members and volunteers so that they could share the campaign.

Having to develop a high level of political understanding and skill 'on the job because we had to', as one group of volunteers told us, was only one aspect. Another was the 'extraordinary financial and managerial abilities' which many reliable observers found in some of the organisations. To become aware of broader issues generally, and especially those which affected the interests of the organisations, was thus a natural next step, and there were many examples of this. One effect was that a large number of individual respondents had grown more interested in politics generally and many of them had become more active. There was circumstantial but strong evidence that it was the systematic long-term schooling in democratic participation at the Arts Centre and its partner,

Pilgrim College, that was responsible for the high degree of active citizenship in that area as measured independently by various forms of participation, including voting percentages. At Boston, Ingleton, in Bassetlaw and at Rugby there was evidence that a notable proportion of local councillors had received their impetus and training in LVOs.

Umbrella groups such as Bassetlaw CVS are in many ways comparable to these others, but also have broader co-ordinating functions in areas where the public services are linked with each other and with the voluntary organisations. Bassetlaw CVS also has the task of administering substantial sums on behalf of the local authority. In effect, it has to be an honest broker within the voluntary sector *and* between it and the whole range of public services. Its members and volunteers therefore have to undertake more complex political learning and a broadly inclusive understanding of the needs and the working methods of all concerned, and of national and regional as well as local political and policy issues.

Responsibility, Skill, Knowledge and Action at National and International Levels

Some of these instances have already been mentioned in earlier sections because the great issues tend to be most fully understood by LVOs in their local context, as when an attack on adult education is felt locally because classes are priced out of public buildings, charged for at fees which are beyond the means of potential students, or disappear altogether. There were a number of instances of individuals (usually elected officers) who had moved on, or added regional and eventually national office and activity to their range. In some organisations imagination and good briefing bridge even larger gaps: the WI Group was raising money to help development work among women in Bangladesh in the intervals of debating potential national resolutions following careful study of evidence. The Singers frequently give concerts away from their base, engage in regular exchanges abroad, and assist other choirs in improving their standards. In the process they have developed an interest in international affairs and contribute to the improvement of relationships at that level. An active interest in national social and economic issues and international relations has been steadily maintained by the Guildhouse since its foundation, and the Wildlife Trust pursues global environmental issues in addition to holding local wildflower censuses and the like. Indeed, environmental issues are a major preoccupation in a number of the organisations.

We have admitted (p. 7 above) that, after satisfying all sampling requirements, we chose successful and exemplary organisations for our sample wherever we could. It is therefore not surprising that some of them have accumulated the kind of expertise which makes them sought after by others from elsewhere in the country and occasionally abroad, who wish to set up similar organisations, or are experiencing difficulty in existing ones. They also tend to provide officers and committee members for national organisations of their congeners where these exist. In acting as consultants or sources of encouragement and stimulus to new endeavour, these organisations contribute in important ways to the development of the voluntary sector generally.

Some Illustrations

Looked at from a personal perspective the four divisions of this section are a single continuum. This may be clarified by concluding with some individual histories which are partly verbatim, partly abbreviated from verbatim accounts:

("A" originally came for help after marriage breakdown and to train for work, then volunteer community worker, trained for this, now unemployed and back as volunteer.) 'It's a place where you could grow ... It changed my life and helped me to find inner strength ... It's given me a sense of my own worth, that I could do things ... I value myself now ... I don't have to prove anything to anybody any more ... I learned to like myself ... I'm much more able to accept other people as they are.'

("B" is a middle-aged woman who came for literacy and later learned to type. She now does voluntary typing and jobs around the office.) 'Because of what I'm doing here I find out about the social problems there are in the area and the facilities, what's available and the organisations around the place. I've become involved ... I'm more socially aware of what's going on locally ... things you don't really think about.'

("C" is a 20-year-old, from a refugee family, currently unemployed. Seems to be here full-time, mainly voluntarily and partly paid, working in a training project for people with learning difficulties and youth club.) She has learned 'how to deal with people'. Coping with racism in the area, including crises which can be serious and involve the safety of people. Has learned to shoulder 'enormous responsibility ... trusted to use own judgment on the spur of the moment in situations which are often explosive.' Learned 'a different kind of patience' in work with trainees: looking out for problems before they arise, 'teaching people routines slowly ... teaching people to learn and become independent ... finding the balance for each of them, not pushing too far but challenging enough.' Has intelligent appreciation of the way both projects on which she works depend especially on local authority policy and decision. Takes continual interest in these, participates in deputations about cuts in youth work and takes some members along with her. Has addressed Council on the subject.

("D" is 27, a student and volunteer. Came seven years ago from Jamaica to marry, now has two children. Has taken English and Maths at the Settlement, is becoming a registered child minder and preparing to study for NNEB. From studying she became a volunteer: organises outings, teaches ABE, serves on equal opportunities steering group, represents the Settlement as member or adviser on several other LVOs. Chair of her local tenants' association and family centre.) A 'definite passion to serve my local community'. 'Trying to make it more open and friendly.' A very strong civic consciousness fuelled by desire to serve and help rather than get her dues. But aware that there is a link to career planning and the CV.

("E" is a full-time teacher on the Settlement's education project. Volunteer prior to extensive professional training.) The need for involvement, learning to make relationships, assertion, political awareness in the sense of knowing and pursuing rights '... Students become involved in fund-raising and grant-saving campaigns, which means they learn about local government and its decision making processes.' 'Quite a few become active citizens' and at least one of the ABE students moved on to office in a tenants' association, subsequently became a local councillor.

Personal and Organisational Characteristics, and Political Learning

Few individual characteristics seem to influence the degree of learning and change in this category. Age, TEA and occupation seem to play no significant part, but sex does in one important respect: women have benefited significantly more than men in learning to advocate, speak, and take action at all levels. On the other hand organisational characteristics play a considerable part in the area of political learning.

All seven categories of organisational objectives (cf. the matrix) are very influential indeed in the area of acquiring an awareness of social issues. Organisations with sociableness as their primary objective are the weakest, but even these score positive responses from almost half their members. Women's organisations and advocacy score almost 100%, and all the rest between these extremes are very strong indeed. On political awareness, advocacy, speaking and action the returns are almost equally strong. Learning is relatively weak only in the sociable organisations and – surprisingly – those concerned with care and health. It is, again, very strong indeed in the women's organisations, and strong in the rest.

The size of organisations, their level of staffing (none, small, medium or large) and that of their external funding (as for staffing) all produce curiously analogous results, with few exceptions. Where size is concerned, while all returns of political learning are high, it is most prominent in the small organisations and becomes less so as they grow in size. Political awareness and learning are highest in LVOs which have no staff and the level of this kind of learning diminishes as staff are introduced and their numbers rise. There is a slight difference with external funding, where the level of political learning is highest with groups receiving none and with those receiving most, with the rest in between.

It seems that all these indications tend in the same direction: the more fully members of LVOs depend upon their own efforts, with neither fellow members nor staff or outside bodies able to shoulder responsibilities for them, the greater their political awareness and learning. The exception are the few LVOs with relatively substantial external funding. Here awareness is high, probably because these organisations depend

absolutely on relatively large subventions, and have to continually negotiate and lobby for them.

Personal Learning and Development

Meaning of the Evidence

Apart from the issue of transmission, to be considered at the end of this
chapter, two major topics related to individual learning and change remain to be addressed. One is the presentation of evidence on the subject
of personal learning, defined as that "which seemed *to the respondents
concerned* to have affected, or changed them *personally* in ways that
seemed significant to them" (p. 52f. above). The other is the question
whether some kind of coherent pattern may emerge from the different
kinds of individual learning and change which form the subject of this
chapter. These two topics of personal learning, and a possible inclusive
interpretation of the individual learning experiences which form the sub-
stance of the chapter as a whole, lend themselves to an attempt at integration.

It seems inevitable this can only be practicable in a context of holistic
psychological approaches, with their parallelism between other aspects
of personal development and learning. These lead from relatively lower
order experiences to those variously identified as "individuation" by
Jung, the achievement of "identity" by Erikson, Maslow's "self-actualisation" or Carl Rogers' "fully functioning". Whether one accepts such in-
terpretations or not, one may at least assume support for the view that
adult learning and development operate at different levels, and that their
aim should be to enable individuals to discover, pursue and, so far as
possible, achieve whatever happens to be their potential. This section
will therefore seek to show that the evidence of personal learning can be
interpreted as a progressive sequence which culminates in whatever is,
for each person, self-discovery of a high order.

The Evidence in Sequential Order

There was a small number of respondents who initially regarded themselves as unaffected by the experience of membership, though probing
more often than not led them to revise that estimate in some such way as
'every time you come you learn something ... keeps your mind busy ... I
may be more affected than I know ... there's an influence there that's in a
way unconscious ...' Others, no less than the research team, were aware
of the fact that everyone is subject to such a variety of influences that it is
impossible to isolate the effects of membership from the rest. Respondents were nevertheless clear about the impact, and it is *their* testimony
which is reported, not the researchers'.

There was massive evidence for the development of a sense of security and basic confidence, and the ability to give and take: 81% reported
increased confidence, 65% gained a stronger sense of achievement or
competence and 43% said they had become better at co-operating. The

evidence is so repetitive that it is only selectively reported here. Much of that from the Gardeners began with the habits of sharing and co-operation, the development of a high degree of mutual trust. They had also learned to meet the requirement of regularity and routine in their activity and to support each other in this. In effect, they had become more organised and had developed a personally meaningful (as opposed to externally imposed and accepted) pattern in their way of life. A number of others, for instance in the self-help groups, spoke of learning to be more organised in order to pursue their interest. All this was felt to be a powerful source of personal confidence.

Almost all respondents began by stressing that growth or recovery of simple and general personal confidence was their first and most important gain from the experience of membership. On that foundation they had learned to build greater self-reliance, initially in the context of the organisation's activities, and an ability to assert themselves there. This, as several of the Widows and members of other women's groups especially reported, was subsequently transferred to other relationships and activities. It was a man, though, who drew the careful distinction by describing his 'new self' as *'confidently* assertive': he felt he could afford to stop whistling in the dark.

On this foundation other changes could develop, all of which contributed to the respondents' or their fellow-members' sense of security. Tolerance and patience were valued highly: 'you know that you aren't going to be laughed at', learn how to understand other people's limitations, to cope constructively with difficult fellow-members but also to recognise and respect their ideas and talents. Confidence means that within the group one can become more outspoken and 'stand up for one's opinion', but tolerate disagreement. A notable number of women told us that they had 'changed so much (they had) learned to stand up to (their) husbands' very different views'; equal discussion was now a feature of their partnerships. A number of husbands, and wives, confirmed this development.

From confidence often followed the assumption of responsibility within the group, and the discharge of this was found to reinforce confidence. As a result respondents were becoming more willing to commit themselves. This was illustrated both by activity (for instance helping others) and, more demandingly, by being '... more open. In the group we can open up, people reveal themselves.' Demanding no less confidence than this, there is the modesty of a prominent Residents' Association member: 'you must be able to listen, the more consultation the less frustration ... you've got to be able to say to yourself, I may be wrong.'

Learning to make and to accept commitment, to care and be cared for, is the next stratum of our evidence. Confidence enables people to begin to look, think and feel beyond themselves. They told us they had become more sensitive to others, that they 'notice and see more' and that 'behind everybody there are lots of problems and worries'. A member of Fifty-Plus, with its built-in sense of the mutability of life, spoke of the prevalence of loneliness and grief among the membership: 'it's made me more aware of the impact of tragedy on people's lives, and how much help we can give them by being there.' 'Being confident' meant being able to forget about self, to listen to people for their own sakes, and accept them. Belonging had made several respondents more concerned for other people, more outgoing, and also more confident and competent at relationships, jobs, activities; it had 'broadened my outlook'.

Women from every kind of organisation told us with the utmost regularity that mutual caring had 'saved (their) sanity' while they were at home with small children and had rebuilt their confidence and competence in adult relationships. Widows spoke of a parallel experience, and school teachers (men especially) seemed, invariably, to find their entry into confident *adult* relationships through voluntary organisations: 'being among my peers came as a great relief to me, being totally honest and free', as one of them said. All spoke of the importance to them of the sense of involvement and of success won through the group. One of the Volunteer Drivers, redundant and in poor health previously, had regained personal confidence through his sense of doing a useful job well, and in consequence his health improved.

The enabling power of solidarity showed up strongly among members of various self-help groups. The Widows have been mentioned. The Macular SH and Arthritis SH members spoke of mutual care and the sharing of problems overcoming the sense of isolation which suffering imposes, boosting confidence, a sense of personal worth and the determination to feel in charge of oneself and of life. Optimism grows, or at least constancy in endurance, and a capacity for enjoyment is recovered within the group's togetherness.

Here again the level of commitment affects outcomes. Difficult youngsters, given responsibility, had 'become pillars of society' in one place. Commitment to more specific learning plays the same part: 'I must have led a very narrow existence prior to that ... it opened my eyes to realities' and led to action on the implications. It became generally clear that the assumption of responsibility or commitment, regardless of the specifics, had given respondents a sense of being stretched, of growing. This seemed particularly evident in the rapid growth in personal stature as well as professional expertise of very young staff members suddenly pitched into senior responsibilities, but also the moving words of an elderly caretaker in an organisation where he was treated and trusted as an equal by professional staff. In that same organisation, a part-time staff member almost doubled his paid hours voluntarily; he felt 'deeply embedded in the place because it's so positive' and a young volunteer assistant reported her deep satisfaction in doing well what she wanted to do, and in being trusted and appreciated. Another respondent summed it up: for him commitment and caring meant 'something to live for, something to do for others' which had made him more tolerant and 'a better person to live with'.

With security, mutual acceptance and caring it becomes possible – bearable perhaps – to develop some degree of self-knowledge, to learn what are one's own strengths and weaknesses. Fifty-Plus, for instance, contributes companionship, contact, new interests, caring, variety of opportunities. It broadens outlooks, stimulates self-discovery and previously unsuspected talent; 'it's filled up the lives of people who wouldn't know what they'd do.' Observers of it noted, in particular, that men who join (even more than women) 'are stretched for what is often the first time', discover potential they have never before used and rapidly develop new skills and new pleasures. 'As an organisation they open up the possibilities of self-discovery for a wide range of people.'

For a substantial proportion of respondents from this organisation it has also meant substantial learning of new roles. 'It's been difficult, interesting, and the result's a great growth of confidence' and 'I feel more confident and more competent in all my undertakings now.' A local doctor more than confirmed respondents' claims and spoke of evidence that 'they're healthier as a result' because 'the more you do for other people the healthier you are ... it leads to all-round well-being' regardless of whether it's physical or mental activity because people who take part in such activities together and assume responsibility of any kind 'become a much more rounded whole'.

Secure confidence, feeling in charge and being able to pursue interests, suggest that people are becoming autonomous. Calm confidence in an ability to cope with life, of holding and being on top of responsibilities, gave some members, for instance of the NWR Group, their sense of independence being won, of the group having become a springboard. Alternatively, to a committee member of a community association 'it means much to be serving the community ... there is real contentment ... you're no longer alone.' A Playgroup member has a strong sense of achievement and has learned that 'there aren't a lot of things I can't do', just as an observer notes of Mountain Rescue members their 'notable growth in self-confidence and in personal authority and self-sufficiency'. Mutual support also frees Writers 'to have faith in myself', gives them 'the courage to take risks'.

The discovery of one's own ability was found, repeatedly, to cause 'a tremendous feeling of satisfaction'. This respondent had learned to accept her own strengths and her weaknesses, and the capacity to lead others which had burst upon her almost as a kind of revelation: from sheer terror in facing people she had learned to *enjoy* the advocacy on behalf of the Widows which she was undertaking. Whatever the particular development, the opportunities which LVOs provided for their members to exercise their talents and skills bred in them confidence in their own competence, or management skills, or encouraged them to explore broader horizons. From these grew not just achievement within the group but the ability to achieve quite generally: this was further evidence that people were becoming autonomous. Here, again, this seemed to be even more important for women than for men, enabling them to resist and eventually to defeat what one called the 'universal pressure on women to keep down'. The case histories on p. 76f. above illustrate this.

'It's been quite a struggle to be me' is the way in which one woman from an economically and socially privileged background explained an odyssey by which she had 'become a completely different person' because of the demanding responsibilities and the cultural opportunities which her LVO had offered her, together with support and esteem for her successful competence. Her sense of achievement rested on intangibles; the tangible rewards of Gardeners produced a similar sense of achievement: 'I feel good, you can see what you've done ...' and this engenders a sense of esteem by fellow members, and of personal worth. 'If you're good at growing something you're looked up to, people ask you how to grow it.' Most members of this LVO were either retired or had been made redundant and 'when out of work you have a sense of not being part of the community, not contributing, no responsibility'. For them allotment gardening becomes a new source of identity and personal worth.

This sense of discovery of one's "real identity" is not easily defined but nevertheless real. Does a Patients' Support member who is, by definition, a former psychiatric patient, belong in this, the foregoing or the next category? 'I'm changed because I'm more caring, realise we all need an interest and to be supported. The help you give to members makes you confident you can cope with your own problems. We know what the others have been through. The most important thing is serenity. You get confident that you're in control ...' Surely such hard-won autonomy is also an achievement of identity or of full potential. 'A kind of fulfilment' is one way in which one of the Archaeologists describes the experience. A Volunteer Drivers' office helper gives a more dynamic account: '... ready to try new things ... never had confidence to try before ... not had confidence to learn anything.' She had now plucked up confidence to 'go to night school ... make my own decisions.' She 'came to give my life meaning' and had succeeded.

Respondents vary in their powers of expression and the vehicles of achievement. A member of the NWR Group found it 'changed my perception of myself and my personality ... has caused me to feel much more like a whole human being', while a member of Fifty-Plus spoke of the loneliness of old age and need for 'non-threatening company': mutual awareness and tolerance led to him 'learning to *be*' and countering the impatience of old age.

Sometimes the experience has an almost visionary quality about it and some respondents found words and images for it which distinguished its special character. Perhaps the most unusual was that of the initiator of a major project who woke in the night, convinced he had heard a voice calling him to launch it. There were others who felt similarly driven, or transformed, like the member of the Widows' SH who had felt helpless, whose commitment developed in her the inner force to become a major leader, advocate and almost agitator. Membership of Kelvedon WEA 'slots all things together in life' or, for another, 'has broken down old assumptions and prejudices and expanded our lives and helped us ... it's made it impossible for us to remain rigid.' Long involvement in study, activity and responsibility at the Guildhouse has 'imbued (an elderly man) with a sense of stirring, a quest' and responsibilities for finance and planning at Ingleton CA have enabled an unskilled operative to fulfil himself as an outstanding administrator and planner. In effect, membership in all kinds of organisations can cause 'an intense desire always to follow up', and people such as one of the Midland Railway members discover the unknown and unexpected potential in themselves, the 'something that wants to do a little bit more ... it lifts you up.'

One of the Mountain Rescue members distinguishes between his earlier motives, rooted in personal adventure, and its later transformation that 'makes you think more deeply about things, about the self-sacrifice of team building', the strain and trauma of injury and death, and 'focuses the mind on things: life, the world'. Indeed, several of this group of interviews are so moving that the temptation to reproduce them is hard to resist. This is hardly surprising, because rescue work with its built-in demands and extremes has the 'attraction of dealing with the unknown; you're more alert ... stretched mentally and emotionally.' It forces the members to develop and grow, to get closer to their potential, to 'be more intensely alive'.

Pigeon Fanciers may be less articulate than this, but speak near-poetry when they describe the same experience: 'you feel lifted; you see their wings close and they sail towards the lofts.' 'When you see the birds coming in at the end of a race you feel lifted, and when you win you feel great...' 'Pigeons are for some their whole life.' Archaeologists can feel that their work puts them in touch with 'something far more deeply interfused' – the seemingly unconscious quotation is interesting. The Singers, with their endless striving for a new perfection just beyond their present capacity, find fulfilment in this more often and with greater pride than in the rare kind of reward of it that appears to have swept them and their audience into a kind of near-visionary state while performing in a great cathedral on the Continent.

What all the responses under this heading have in common is a sense that learning and change of this order are regarded as permanent and affecting people's personal attitudes and behaviour. Evidence of personal learning, such as that which has been recounted here, may be recorded without comment or interpretation. When considered in the sequence in which it has been presented, the idea obtrudes itself that it may be linked to theories of the satisfaction of personal needs, or to some kinds of religious or other ideological hierarchies. The notion of a hierarchy of achievement and increasing fulfilment of potential is, indeed, hard to resist, even if it is expressed in terms of "added value".

Personal Learning and Personal and Organisational Characteristics

Personal learning tends to vary substantially according to some personal characteristics, though age does not figure in our evidence here. Confidence growing out of a sense of achievement and competence, of defeating time, links very closely indeed with age in the obvious instance of Fifty-Plus, but this is not sufficient to affect the overall statistics. The Trenaman effect shows up again (masking the special cases which were discussed earlier) in that very high incidence of the sense of discovering, and achieving, a higher personal potential which seems largely to move in step with TEA.

When women and men are compared, equal proportions discover and achieve this same higher potential. Men have a highly significant greater sense of achievement from this than women. In every other respect the women's responses show more learning and greater development than are claimed by the men, at a highly significant level. Women developed more confidence from a low level, learned to deploy their skills more confidently, were more aware of experiencing greater esteem as a result, and increased their sense of independence and autonomy.

Organisational variables seemed to have a similar impact as in the area of political learning. There are more and greater personal changes and learning recorded from small and medium sized than medium to large LVOs and, generally speaking, the same is true of those which employ no paid staff. The reason is probably not that staff prevent learning but that staff are to be found in large organisations and that these, being few, show up less in the overall statistics.

Organisational objectives revealed considerable differences. Generally speaking personal learning and change were greatest in physical activities (100%), and very high indeed in personal interests, women's organisations, care and health. They were least in sociable ones. Awareness of a sense of one's achievements and the development of competence were distributed in much the same way. The sense of having and achieving a higher potential surfaced most strongly in interest-based and physical activities and increased independence in women's organisations, physical activities and care and health.

Transmission of Individual Learning

Speaking of the total effect of belonging to his particular LVO, one respondent summed up the process: 'You can't help but reflect it ... you're the sum of your experiences ... you share, you pass on, discuss, influence others all the time'. This is no doubt true, but it was far more difficult to gather sound evidence for the transmission of individual learning and change than for its original impact. This is hardly surprising in view of the fact that what had affected respondents most, and was therefore likely to be transmitted most powerfully, was hardest to grasp and express in words addressed to an interviewer. It is also likely that the transmission of experience is less common and powerful than its original impact. Nevertheless it happens on a substantial scale: 61% of members claim to have passed outcomes of membership on to family members, and 72% to friends and neighbours, with lesser proportions at greater distance. Between 20% and 28% had been stimulated to contact various arms and services of local government, and rather less of them national equivalents and the media.

Members of inward-looking groups were the most active transmitters at personal levels; members of generalist and outward-looking ones were more active than specialists in contacting local and national government. A highly significant, and interesting, statistic shows minimum-TEA respondents to be the most frequent transmitters where the relationship is personal, and least frequent in their contacts with other people in the area, and the local media. However, distinctions between different areas such as social, content, etc. learning inevitably made less sense to respondents than to interviewers. The evidence will therefore be divided into two very broad groups only; transmission to close associates and more distant transmission.

Transmission to Close Family and Friends

By far the most frequent response was concerned with overcoming loneliness or isolation. This was true not just of groups which aimed at it, such as Fifty-Plus with its elderly and often widowed membership, but quite generally. Belonging to any LVO means the extension of people's social network and their sense of belonging, and this was mentioned more often as being shared with spouses, and others, than any other effect. In some instances it was seen as a definite form of social education for husbands, overcoming 'male isolationism' and above all teaching men to bear a fairer share of household and family duties while enabling wives to attend meetings of the LVO. Partnerships were becoming more equal.

There was some evidence, too, of sons learning, sometimes painfully but occasionally with enthusiastic support, that mothers had roles and needed space as individuals apart from their familial role, or could develop new ones. Daughters not uncommonly picked up interests and commitments from their mothers and followed them into membership. Sons tended to follow fathers, but less often, and then in specialised activities such as gardening and pigeon fancying. A significant number of the elderly Guildhouse respondents were second generation members, but none of these appeared to have involved their own offspring. The growth of mobility and a wider range of opportunities may be responsible for this.

However, generational succession was a significant element in Archaeology, the Railway Trust, Pigeon Fancying, Gardening, possibly with the Singers, and very strongly at Ingleton CA. The first four of these are highly demanding specialised commitments, while Ingleton CA, as an umbrella organisation, includes all the activities available in a small isolated community. It would be impracticable there for children not to be involved in something under the same umbrella. It is significant, however, that a notable number of the sons and daughters of the most active members have founded comparable organisations elsewhere on removal.

At a more straightforward level of transmission the effects of the Playgroup and the PTA need no explanation except for the former's impact on husbands. Respondents commonly found themselves sharing with their spouses the content of discussion groups and WEA classes week by week. This was particularly evident in the case of the two women's groups (WI and NWR) and the active WEA branch. In all three learning and interests were systematically and regularly passed on to avid listeners at home and discussed late into the night. The extramural activities of women's groups (theatre visits, various forms of sport, etc.) were fully shared with husbands, whose cultural range grew accordingly. Husbands were also persuaded to join other groups, such as parent-teacher associations, or taken on rambles. LVOs seem to be a particularly effective method of stimulating non-member husbands to emulate the greater cultural adventurousness of their womenfolk. The process can sometimes lead to major change: one wife took pride from the fact that her husband who, previously, 'wouldn't say boo to a goose' was now leading two LVO groups. However, there were also instances where a wife's personal development had led to the break-up of marriages which had not been strong in the first instance.

Probably the process went farthest in particularly strong generalist organisations such as Ingleton CA or the WI Group, with whole families becoming activated across a wide range of involvement from the personal to the economic and political spheres, and their friends and neighbours being roped in. There was mention of several daughters in turn becoming competent political operators. The impact on the families of strongly specialist groups has been mentioned. In one such instance (the Singers) this is widely extended through home, neighbourhood and work-based friendship to create a supporters' network which sells tickets, attends concerts, does chores, and receives a substantial musical education in the process.

More Distant Transmission

The Singers' experience leads naturally to other instances of more distant transmission. Teacher members regularly use at school both musical and human relations skills they have learned in the group. Concerts and informal links with other choirs, including the loan of individual members to them for concerts, influence musical standards in the region, and regular international exchanges do so in that of their foreign partners. Ingleton CA, Fifty-Plus, Widows' SH, Railway Trust and Bassetlaw CVS had all influenced or even spawned similar organisations regionally, nationally and, once or twice, internationally. The Settlement was said by other LVOs and the public services to be a powerful influence not just on these organisations' staffs and volunteers, but on the whole ethos and content of their operations.

As many as 23% of respondents passed their interests or experience on to people in their work community. Teachers had recruited colleagues in the crucial developmental stages at Ingleton; archaeologists did so in their varied jobs; Mountain Rescue members were usually first-aiders at work as well as dealing with accidents and crises of every kind in their villages; Volunteer Drivers were teaching friends and neighbours as well as their families about the needs of the old and disabled and the benefits to them and to the community if they were helped to be mobile.

Several members of the Wildlife Trust found that their interest had a direct influence on their work and enabled them to fire new people with their own enthusiasm. This included not just librarians, teachers, wildlife artists and booksellers but also a travelling salesman and a doctor. Members of the Arts Centre were using the centre and their own learning there with school children, and at work of every kind. Individual visitors and groups or businesses hiring rooms are confronted with exhibitions and notices of activities in the lobby and coffee bar and much varied good talk in the bar: there is evidence that many are influenced and discover new interests.

At a deeper level it is more a matter of attitudes which are communicated – of openness, energy and social commitment as at Sibsey or Ingleton, of courageous persistence as with the Widows, of sheer professionalism as with the Railway Trust. A surprising proportion of Guildhouse respondents felt they had absorbed personal attitudes and philosophies, and inter-personal skills, from the example of a late warden. They had translated these into comparable staff relationships at their work places. Several of the Kelvedon WEA members told us of applying the disciplines of study and the skills of group discussion and group democracy to a varied assortment of jobs. And Mountain Rescue members found that the searching experience of that task was 'bound to have an influence on how I deal with other people' – whether they happened to be managers in training, hill-walkers, office-workers or teachers.

Chapter 6

Individual Learners and Group Types

The previous chapter gave our findings about the learning and development experienced by individual members of LVOs. The next addresses the learning and development of the LVOs themselves. This leaves, between them, a gap which is not very wide, but needs to be bridged. What is at issue here is the question whether the participation and related behaviour of individuals are affected by the kinds of groups which they join. Is there evidence that this may be so? Or could the evidence point the opposite way, suggesting that certain kinds of individuals are attracted to given kinds of LVOs? Superficially expressed, do the content and characteristics of groups change those who join them, or do personal characteristics predicate group choice? Or, crudely, do organisations choose people or people organisations? Are both versions true? More than elsewhere in the project, field experience and intuition can answer such questions: this chapter presents the evidence for a complex syndrome.

Findings from the Questionnaire Data Base

Participation

A manual analysis of the individual questionnaires was carried out while the main data base was being created. It immediately confirmed a suspicion which had been growing during the interview programme. This was that the development over a course of years of respondents' participation in all forms of learning and other leisure activities varied distinctly according to whether they were members of specialist or generalist groups. When these variations were plotted against organisational objectives they led to the establishment of two group types, the generalist and the specialist. The behaviour of members had varied consistently according to the kind of group to which they belonged. Attempts to find parallel distinctions or polarities, such as between learning and sociable leisure activities, led to no significant way of explaining the variation.

All respondents to the questionnaire took part in other activities in addition to their particular LVO, ranging from just one to as many as 21. Three-quarters of respondents listed between three and 10. However, if they are divided according to whether they belong to specialist or generalist organisations, and moderately (1–8) or strongly (9–21) participative, a highly significant pattern emerges. This demonstrates the very different habitual approaches to other interests and activities which were found among members of specialist and generalist LVOs, with men swinging towards specialist groups and women to generalist ones. Another, fascinating, aspect of this set of correlations is that the low activity (1–8) and high activity (9–21) groups break in opposite directions: lower participation rates and specialist tendency go together, as opposed to high participation and generalism. This, in turn, links with the already known tendencies of women towards generalism and men to specialism.

Diagram 12 (cp. Table 3): Participation rates, type of group, and sex

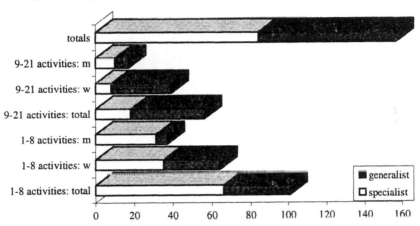

The focus is sharpened further by looking at the ways in which the respondents' habits of participation had changed over a number of, and sometimes many years. Less than a quarter of those who widened their participation to other interests over the years were members of specialist LVOs, and only two of the 73 generalists reduced their interests. The large proportion of women members in generalist groups, whose participation widens, is especially noteworthy:

Diagram 13 (cp. Table 4): History of participation, by type of group, and sex (%) (N=157)

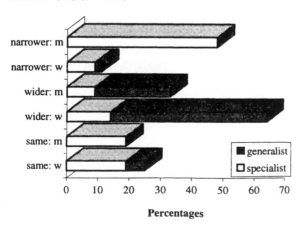

Percentages

This analysis reveals two contrasting types of participative behaviour. Members of specialist LVOs tend, more often than not, to have started with a moderate number of activities and interests. This diminishes on joining those which most effectively meet their needs, until it reaches a stable minimum. This includes the specialist organisation of their choice and, maybe, one or a few others which pursue the same or related objectives. Extreme examples are individuals who had a broad spectrum of involvement some time ago, but now belong to two or three wildlife-oriented societies and classes. Others may belong to a chamber choir and perhaps a quartet, but have given up links with large choirs and wider interests beyond.

Members of generalist LVOs tend towards the converse history. Having joined the organisation of their choice, they discover new interests and gradually expand their range of pursuits and learning activities. Kelvedon WEA (with a high proportion of women members), or WI Group members, exemplify this; their core activity has sent them off in many and varied directions but seems, nevertheless, to hold as a central commitment. The actual rate of participation varied widely and ranged up to 21 – admittedly among retired individuals. Women and men differ distinctly, with women much more likely to expand their repertoire than men, and to have higher participation rates. This coincides with their greater tendency to join generalist organisations.

Terminal Education Age, Sex and Participation

It was natural to enquire whether initial cycle educational experience (TEA) correlated with either the contrasting groups or with participation rates within them, or if there were any other significant factors. The details of TEA are known for 154 of the 157 questionnaire returns, but these returns are not representative of the overall interview sample. In particular they include a higher proportion of those whose initial education went beyond the minimum. In addition, respondents with a minimum TEA include a small but disproportionate number who subsequently became mature students. Nevertheless the small but equal numbers of women and men in the minimal category are striking. However, since there are almost twice as many returns from women the proportions represented by these equal numbers differ notably. On the other hand women are very much more heavily represented than men in the intermediate TEA group. This may be a reason for the curious fact that the intermediate TEA group displays a strikingly higher propensity to learn, change and participate responsibly than the 20-plus group:

Diagram 14 (cp. Table 5): TEA and sex of respondents

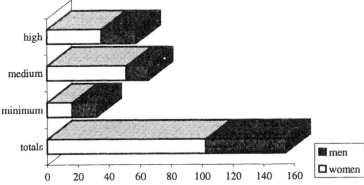

Educational background seems to play very little part in the choice of specialist or generalist organisations. It is, however, very noticeable that most women with a TEA above the minimum participate in a large number of activities. This trend is confirmed by considering the responses in the context of the case study groups. The LVOs where participation is wide among most or all members are the NWR and WI Groups, Kelvedon WEA, Fifty-Plus and Gorgie Dalry Writers. The first four are generalist groups and only the last is specialist. Those LVOs whose questionnaire returns show their members to be narrowing their activities are Mountain Rescue, Archaeologists and Singers – all specialists. There had been no significant changes in the Playgroup and Wildlife Trust members' participation rates. Within this somewhat selective group there is thus outstandingly strong evidence that women are more inclined than men to join generalist organisations, and to expand their range of participation. This was subsequently confirmed to a highly significant degree from the main data base.

Chicken or Egg?

These findings do not enable us to state whether these contrasting behaviours are caused by the kind of interests people have, and the organisations they join, or if individuals discover their essential bent through the processes of membership and then join or resign accordingly. The evidence seems to point in the second direction because the questionnaires show that expansion or concentration usually follow upon entry into the LVO concerned. However, there are exceptions showing a more gradual development whose beginning precedes membership of the LVO from which they respond. It seems very likely, therefore, that both solutions to the conundrum are correct, but that the balance varies individually.

Findings from the Main Data Base

Some Cross-Correlations

Having established a relationship between specialism and concentration and generalism and expansion, the question arises whether there are other relationships which are analogous. Is there more learning and development, or a different balance between different kinds of learning, when we compare dynamic with static or divergent LVOs (cf. Glossary)? And how do these findings compare with those of a parallel statistical analysis of the contrasts between generalist and specialist groups?

It will, perhaps, come as no surprise that the results from the two sets of calculations are almost precisely the same, although the overall distribution of the sexes differs. Overall, they divide roughly equally between generalist and specialist groups. In the dynamic/static comparison, however, the imbalance between the sexes is highly significant, with 60% of women respondents in dynamic groups and 55% of men in static or divergent. There are also equally marked differences as regards social and personal learning. 'Learning to accept and be accepted', 'developing deeper relationships' and 'learning to accept commitment', increases in confidence and 'ability to function independently', or 'achieve a higher potential' – all these are much more strongly represented in both the dynamic and the generalist groups than in the static/divergent and the specialist ones. The same applies to content and other more specific learning, including 'taking more responsibility', discussion skills and 'improving inter-personal skills'. On the other hand specialist group members claimed a much stronger record of learning to co-operate than their opposite numbers.

Well over half the members spoke of various kinds of occupational benefits associated with membership of their LVOs, but the only comparison of any interest was in the area of learning to be more systematic and to plan ahead. Here the specialist and the static organisations took a highly significant lead over the generalist and the dynamic ones, probably because of the strongly marked incidence of this benefit among allotment holders, pigeon fanciers and archaeologists.

The parallelism between the two pairs of categories broke down completely in the area of political learning, where there were no significant differences between dynamic and static groups. On the other hand the generalist group members differed from the specialists at a highly significant level in their greater awareness of broad social issues and of political implications, and in having become involved in various forms of political action on behalf of their organisations and their objectives. This was confirmed by observers.

We next enquired whether the contrast between inward- and outward-looking LVOs would produce the same information about learning as the generalist-specialist division. There was, for instance, strong evidence that members of inward-looking groups claimed social learning gains. Conversely, more members of outward-looking groups claimed content learning gains. Would staffing or group size or group objectives affect the outcome? It was clearly necessary to pursue these questions with the more powerful assistance of the main data base.

The findings from this source which have been reported in this subsection have proved to compare closely to the questionnaire results. The use of this material in answering the questions posed in the last paragraph is therefore justifiable. It became clear at an early stage that analysis according to group size would not furnish any significant results, and this was abandoned. The three areas which were explored in detail were the relationship of individuals and groups against the existence and numbers of staff, inward- or outward-looking objectives, and whether the group was dynamic, static or divergent. For the purpose of the last of these explorations, those static groups which had proved to be borderline candidates for the divergent category were added to it, as in Chapter 3 (cf. p. 35 above). For each of these three areas, individual learning and development in its five categories was cross-tabulated with the given group characteristic.

Members' Learning and the Staffing of Groups

Two general points need to be borne in mind when considering the findings which follow. One is that *everyone learns* and is aware of it, no matter in what kind of organisation, including the divergent. Moreover, all do so at a level which is statistically as well as personally significant. The other is that a considerable majority of the unstaffed LVOs (11 of 18) are specialist, and vice versa.

Social learning and development is the only category which does *not* produce significant differences between groups with or without staff. In content learning members of organisations without staff show greater improvement in discussion skills than the others. Most of these belong to specialist groups, which mediate more specific content. However, they also include three strong generalist but discussion-based groups without staff (Kelvedon WEA and the NWR and WI Groups). Members of staffed groups claim greater gains of occupational learning than their opposite numbers. The greatest differences occur in political and personal learning. Members of unstaffed groups become more aware and involved politically, especially as concerns broader social issues. In the area of personal learning and change they show greater gains in confidence and self-possession arising from the development of relationships, and also a greater development of personal autonomy. On the other hand a higher proportion of members of staffed LVOs feel that they are working at a higher personal potential.

Members' Learning and the Outward–Inward Divide

These findings, too, are clear-cut. Members of inward-looking LVOs show significantly higher levels of learning and change in one aspect of social learning, that of ability to bring about social contact. In the occupational field they are far ahead of the others in becoming more systematic and planning their activities. In every other respect members of outward-looking groups are significantly more successful. They claim higher levels of acceptance and tolerance and interpersonal skills generally. They have acquired higher levels of organising skill, ability to accept responsibility, and to co-operate. Their occupations benefit more from their LVO membership and vice versa. They have developed a higher level of awareness of broad political and social issues, and they are more conscious of being esteemed and their activities being appreciated in the group.

Altogether, then, members of outward-looking groups seem better at working with others and at taking on responsibility. They feel more integrated and confident, and their social skills and attitudes are appreciated by others. They show stronger evidence of active citizenship.

This degree of polarisation seems odd until one considers which organisations are in the inward and outward groups. The latter, with one very small exception, consists of two tightly-knit sub-groups. One contains four LVOs, with few (one of them relatively so) members. These four will be found (in Chapter 8) categorised as having negative or neutral effects. The other sub-group embraces six large and effective umbrella LVOs whose greater numbers overwhelm the other sub-group statistically. There is, indeed, an obvious and very significant statistical difference between inward- and outward-looking organisations, but the causes of these differences seem to lie elsewhere. However clear-cut the findings about learning and the inward-outward divide may be, they are also puzzling. It looks as if any meaning that lies hidden in these particular statistical findings in themselves and in relation to staffing may have been obscured by the individual quality of the organisations in the sample.

Members' Learning and Group Stance

Chapter 8 considers the significance of a division into groups whose stance (at the time of each case study) has been characterised as dynamic, static or divergent (cf. Glossary). This can be usefully applied to the current topic, though without going into detail except to note that here a few static LVOs which were not so much on a plateau as teetering on its edge, have been moved into the divergent category.

The differences between these three groups of LVOs are so great and so consistent that it is necessary to repeat that *everyone* had learned and changed. However, under almost every criterion of social, content, occupational, political and personal learning and change there was the same rank order (1 dynamic, 2 static, 3 divergent) at levels of difference which were never less than significant. Moreover, although the static organisations mostly came second, very high proportions of their members had learned much. It was the degree to which the divergent trailed that was so noteworthy.

There is one instance only where members of the divergent group were ahead of the rest. This was in awareness of issues within their own organisation. Since internal issues are liable to loom large in weak or troubled LVOs this may be expected. Members of static groups edge those of the dynamic out of the lead when it comes to a sense of achievement and competence in their activity, and also in the occupational and political significance of their learning. The first two of these seem logical enough, and due to the close link between specialisation and a static stance. The third seems surprising, and may be due to chance factors.

Some Tentative Conclusions

The statistical findings have been so mutually consistent and have so satisfyingly confirmed each other and the expectations aroused by the field evidence, that one keeps looking for flaws and is grateful for uncertainties. It seems easier therefore to begin with:

What Cannot be Concluded and Why

- No general conclusions are possible as to whether some kinds of members gravitate towards some kinds of organisations, or if the inclinations of some are changed as a result of their membership. Almost certainly this is an individual matter. Certainly, too, both are true and both processes may be operating at the same time in the same individuals. Moreover, there is nothing in our evidence to suggest what personal characteristics point individuals in one direction or another.

- Some of the factors we have isolated are most unlikely to play any significant part in the relationship between individual learning and change and the groups within which they take place. It is virtually certain that group size can be excluded. There are significant differences between groups with and without staff, but staff do not seem to be the element which causes them. They are likely to be due to chance factors such as particular individuals and circumstances affecting particular groups.

The Evidence Does Support Some Conclusions

- There is a definite difference between individuals who tend to join generalist and those who join specialist groups. Their tastes and histories of participation are distinct. Their learning habits and outcomes differ notably in ways that suggest personality differences, which we have not identified.

- There appear to be analogous and similarly clear-cut differences between those who belong to outward-looking and inward-looking groups, but a number of chance organisational factors seem to make the evidence of these differences less clear-cut. It appears that all forms of social and inter-personal learning, together with their satisfactions, are a particular source of attraction in outward-looking groups, and serve as a context in which other learning behaviours are acquired.

- The dynamic–static–divergent division between groups is clear-cut, though it must be remembered that it discriminates between organisations, not people. Dynamic and generalist groups, and static and specialist ones are, respectively, more or less congruent: the dynamic tend to attract mostly generalists and the static mostly specialists. This does not necessarily mean that specialist individuals lack personal dynamism, or that generalists are necessarily endowed with it. In a successful static group the energies of members are directed into ever more intensive activity focused on a single aim or group of aims. A generalist group can only be successfully dynamic if it attracts at least some individuals who pour their enthusiasm into maintenance roles.

- The existence of a pattern is not in doubt, and individuals and group types evolve within it. But it is a complex, multi-dimensional pattern; all its components interact with each other: causality appears to be reciprocal.

- One distinctive set of links is absolutely clear. Women preponderate heavily in dynamic and generalist groups, and men in those which are static and specialist.

Chapter 7

How Do Groups Learn and Change?

A Categorisation of Sample LVOs

Chapter 5 dealt with the kinds of learning and change which individual respondents had experienced and Chapter 6 linked these to certain group characteristics. Here an attempt will be made to consider the LVOs themselves as organisms which are capable of learning and development. In Chapter 3, each of the case study organisations was briefly sketched from the point of view of its objectives and general characteristics. They will now be reconsidered in order to elicit a different set of characteristics: their stance, staffing, structure, and whether specialist or generalist, and inward- or outward-looking.

In the first instance each LVO will be assigned to one of three groups, the dynamic, the static and the divergent. The dynamic are those which, at the time we studied them, were observably learning and developing. Another set appeared to be static in the sense that they were not undergoing any notable changes. The divergent were those which appeared to be in some kind of disadvantageous position in relation to their declared objectives. In addition to this categorisation, any notable learning and change which each of the groups was experiencing or had experienced, will be identified. In this process, as elsewhere, observer comment as well as member and staff evidence will be drawn on. The tripartite categorisation will be checked against the other characteristics of LVOs in order to discover whether there are significant relationships. A kind of map of the ups and downs and flat places of our territory will emerge, and this will act as an introduction to an enquiry into some of the forces which have shaped the land we shall traverse.

One important proviso must be made. Each of our case studies, however searching, was a snapshot. It looked at the LVO concerned at one moment in time, and in the state in which it then happened to be. It could have been static then, or even divergent. To have come into existence at all it must have been dynamic in the past; it may have become so again by the time these words are being drafted. Moreover, it is in the nature of certain activities that they should attain to stasis in order to meet as appropriately as possible whatever are the needs which arise from their objectives. In such groups individuals probably learn and change *because* the organisation is stable. Activities such as pigeon fancying, allotment gardening and perhaps self-help groups which have attained maturity may be examples of this.

It is, indeed, suggested that organisations necessarily pass through a cycle from dynamism to stasis and divergence, resumed dynamism and so on unless they fall victim to terminal regression and dissolution. This cycle of neat predestination is said to have been observed in various organisations. However, we have not observed it in the case studies, since longitudinal studies would be needed. It will be noted in the descriptive categorisation which follows that there are some organisations which have remained dynamic throughout their long lives, and others which attain to and then maintain stasis. All that can be said of those which are firmly divergent is that they show no signs of reverting to dynamism, and would require some kind of internal revolution, probably under external pressures, to change their stance.

The history of organisations in our sample is significant for our purposes because it is at a given moment that we have found group learning and organisational development taking place, or in abeyance, or positively rejected. Moreover, analysis of particular organisations will show that individual and group learning do not necessarily coincide. The balance of a group's actual (as opposed to theoretical) characteristics and objectives can change subtly or even radically following changes in its learning stance.

Any discoverable correlations between objectives and characteristics and the group's stance (dynamic, static or divergent) may therefore be significant. Above all it is essential to resist the temptation to make value judgments by assuming that dynamism necessarily equals growth or size, or success, or that stasis spells dullness, and a move into the divergent category necessarily contraction – though it can, on our evidence, be assumed to equal failure to meet original objectives. A new organisation like Aekta SH is certainly dynamic in the sense that the group is learning and developing, but this does not necessarily mean that it is growing, or that it is at present successful: it is simply too new for any such judgment and much of the energy which makes it dynamic is still provided by a professional worker.

On the other hand it has already been shown that certain organisations need to attain and maintain stasis to succeed; when they meet their objectives they provide a context for individual learning and change, but the organisation itself has ceased to do so, nor would it be to its advantage to become dynamic unless either needs or circumstances change. Other arguments against too much reliance on generalisation arise from the influence of external circumstances and changes of personnel, including members of staff. In any event, what follows is descriptive, and not judgmental.

The case studies are classified, impressionistically, in the three categories and, at the same time, allocated to their appropriate place in the other distinctive categories which we have used. Significant historical information will be briefly noted, including individual or small group effects on the organisation where they are significant, and known to the project:

1. *The NWR Group* is a *generalist* organisation because specifically dedicated to a variety of interests. It is *inward-looking* in the sense that it exists and acts for the benefit of its membership. It has *no staff,* and its structure achieves the *democratic* extreme, by which the group eschews any structure whatever. All responsibility is held in common, with the exception

of the rotating one of programme secretary. This is, of course, practicable only because the group is small, meets in members' homes and therefore has no finances. It means that the group itself had to develop the skills of total participation and shared responsibility both by the group for its members and members for the working of the group. Flexible and innovative programming demands sensitive antennae and the turnover in membership calls for maturity. As the group's programme is by definition changing continuously, and as it introduces its membership to a changing array of extramural activity, it belongs in the *dynamic* category.

2. *Ingleton CA* is *generalist in* view of its range of activities, *outward-looking* because it engages in community development and activity, has *paid staff*, and is *democratically* run, develops continuously, and is therefore *dynamic*. The group learning it and its daughter organisations have undergone since its foundation more than a generation ago is multifarious and readers are referred to Case Study 2 (Elsdon, 1991c). A quick indication of past learning includes the forging of coherent action groups, the creation of constitutions and complex co-operative management structures, planning and construction of buildings and other facilities, commitment to rolling long-term social, educational, physical and financial planning and inter-organisational planning.

3. *The Guildhouse* is *generalist* but *inward-looking* because it serves a particular membership, which any adult can join. It lost its warden post some years ago but employs a small *office staff* and class tutors. It is an effective *democracy*. The organisation's major developmental phase as an institution can be dated a long way back to the tenure of two early wardens. The quality of their personal leadership and influence was high. As a result an institutional identity and capacity for group learning and development emerged which coped with crises, and loss of professional leadership. During the early period the institution also created a number of other major cultural and social organisations serving the town and, as a body, became an acknowledged major force for civic social and cultural development.

Its current programme of classes and activities and the structure of its membership are notably unchanging. Compared with the distant past it might be described as divergent, but *stasis* would be a more accurate description of its current stance. However, the absence of development and the high average age of the membership place fairly obvious limitations upon the continuance of stasis.

4. *The Arts Centre* is *generalist* because of its range, *outward-looking* because its activities and services are aimed at and largely serve the community in general and not only regular members and other participants. It has a *paid staff* and is an effective *democracy*. Its programme and other activities are continually developing and changing and its structures are being adapted accordingly. It belongs in the *dynamic* category although this characteristic is currently less pronounced than it has been in the past. This is due to the recent arrival of new and as yet inexperienced

professional staff. During the preceding interim the voluntary officers carried out management tasks and endeavoured to maintain the organisation's dynamism. The contrast with stasis at the Percival Guildhouse may be due to more recent dynamic leadership and also the energetic originality of some volunteers. Like Ingleton, this is a complex organisation which developed around dynamic individuals. They learned to develop structures into which other groups were able to mesh themselves, and they engaged in coherent planning of social, physical, educational and cultural development. Unlike Ingleton, here the organisation was launched from the base of another LVO, developed in conjunction with it and under shared professional and administrative staffing. Though independent now, the two institutions continue to co-operate closely and between them exert a powerful influence on local civic, social and cultural life through their own provision, through influence upon others and through the political training they provide for citizens at large and for local politicians. Instructive contrasts emerge in the relationships of professional staff to officers and committee, especially in comparison with some other case studies.

5. *The WI Group* is *generalist* and, for statistical purposes, *inward-looking* because its declared objectives are directed at its membership. This is in other ways an inadequate description of an organisation whose members are, with its encouragement, engaged in multifarious services to the community, as shown in the case study (No. 5, in Stewart *et al.*, 1992). It has *no staff*, is *democratic*, with widely dispersed responsibility, and *dynamic*. Starting from a former culture of dependency, deference and autocratic management, the group literally turned itself inside out. It is now a particularly instructive example, on a relatively small scale, of internal group learning of democratic autonomy and effective management, both of current activity and innovation, and the direct transfer of that learning to other groups within the local community and to the life and management of that community itself.

6. *Ujima* had a short but turbulent history. Its aims were *generalist* and it was *outward-directed*. It had *a paid staff* and, theoretically, a *democratic* constitution. It appears at one time to have engaged in some effective advisory and supportive activities with members of ethnic minority communities, and it had organised one careers convention. However, it seems that the leading group was not equipped to manage staff and control funding, which may have been excessive for its stage of development. At the time of the case study the organisation was preoccupied with internal relationships which did not reflect either its objectives or its constitution, and it did not appear that the outward aims were being pursued with much energy or success. It is therefore classed as *divergent*.

7. The *Rotary Club* is, like others of its kind, *generalist* in its objectives and activities, by definition *outward-looking*, has *no staff*, and a *democratic* structure. Perhaps mainly owing to social and economic change in its catchment area its membership is static and its activities are apparently

unchanging. There is evidence of individual learning and development on the part of a few members, but none of group learning; the developmental curve seems to be on the point of turning downwards. The group may still be appropriately placed in the *static* category, but the age range and number of members and the kind and volume of activity undertaken suggest a *divergent tendency.*

8. *The Widows' SH* is *specialist* in that it serves the specific interests of a particular group, and as such *inward-looking.* It has *no staff*, a *democratic* constitution, is organisationally mature, and successfully active in its chosen field, thus mediating substantial individual learning and change. However, it does not seem to be engaged in any noticeable change or developmental activity as a group, though it was so very strongly in the past and individual members are active nationally. It is placed in the *static* category.

9. *Bassetlaw CVS* is *generalist, outward-looking,* has *a paid staff* and a representative *democratic* structure. By definition its function is to act as a source of and a focus for multi-directional communication of ideas, suggestions, policy formation, organisational, social and educational skills and resources. It is thus strongly *dynamic.*

10. *Macular SH* is *specialist, inward-looking* because aimed at its members' condition, *democratic* and has *no staff.* In this early stage of its existence it is learning to develop its programme, activities and structure. It is thus *dynamic.*

11. *Patients' Support* is *specialist.* Its members are themselves former patients like those whom they now support. As a result they happen to benefit substantially from the activity. Nevertheless self-help is here a by-product since the group's objective is to support the current patients who form the council. It is therefore classed as *outward-looking.* It has *no staff*, an informal but *democratic* structure, and the evidence shows learning and development not just on the part of individual members but by the group in handling the delicate relationships with patients and the even more delicate ones with staff. It is therefore *dynamic.*

12. *Arthritis SH* is *specialist, directed inwards* at the needs of its members, has *no staff*; is learning to be *democratic*, and still in its expansive *dynamic* stage.

13. The *Archaeologists* are *specialist, directed inwards* to their members' interests, have *no staff*, and are *democratic.* Their early history is an interesting example of ways in which a highly specialised organisation, led by intensely committed individuals, can shape itself by making systematic use of educational facilities provided from outside by statutory and other sources. It appears currently to be on *a static* (though substantial) plateau

of activity.

14. The *Singers* are *specialist, directed inwards* at their interest, and *democratic*; their public and educational services and the regular involvement of large numbers of supporters are by-products. Because of the formal relationship and payment of a token honorarium to their conductor they are classed as having *paid staff*, although in other ways their conductor could be classed as a specialised kind of member. The group is *dynamic* because engaged in continuous learning and development. It also illustrates the way in which individual learning and change and that of the group are reciprocally related: individual development and co-operation between very individualistic characters are required in order to raise standards and enlarge the scope of the group, and the implicit demands of the group force upon its members substantial commitment, learning, and the suppression of personal traits and desires.

15. The *Railway Trust* attracts very large numbers of the public, whose payments finance its activities, and the local economy as a whole also benefits. Their support pays for the activities. The organisation exists, fundamentally, to serve the passionate interest of its members in all aspects of railways. It is thus *inward-looking* and *specialist*. There are *paid members of staff*, but its structure is *democratic*. There appears to be no evidence of major developmental change of the group as such, but the range of its activities, equipment and lines continues to expand, while the growth of paid staff introduces stresses with which the group must learn to cope. It is therefore more appropriately placed in the *dynamic* than in the static category.

16. *Fifty-Plus* is *generalist, directed inwards* to the needs and interests of its members and has *no paid staff*. It is another example of the predominant influence of individuals in forming a group and giving it particular characteristics. Its structure is theoretically authoritarian or possibly patriarchal. It is thus *undemocratic* and recorded as such, though in spirit informal in the extreme. The organisation is engaged in continuous learning and development by trying to identify and meet new needs in the local community, and also by adapting its structure to future requirements. It has maintained a *dynamic* stance throughout its existence.

17. *The Settlement* is *generalist, outward-looking* to its geographical community, has *paid staff*, and a *democratic* structure. The case study shows groups within it as well as the organisation as a whole to be strongly *dynamic* in two different ways. In the first instance both the Settlement and all its daughter organisations are learning and developing in response to the continually changing balance of social, organisational and personal problems they identify in the community around and in other organisations with which they co-operate. Secondly, they are forced into continual learning and adaptation owing to the stresses imposed on them by central and local government policies and action. As a result dynamism is, in effect, a condition of continued existence, and appears to have been

throughout the organisation's history.

18. The *W London CA* is *generalist*, theoretically *outward-looking*, and has *paid staff*. Its governing structure is theoretically *democratic* and statistically recorded as such, though in practice authoritarian, because the organisation has lost its internal political skills, and allowed authority to fall into the hands of paid staff whose objectives (defined in the self-styled director's words as 'I run a tight ship') do not appear to be in accordance with those of the institution. In the past it had been an effectively democratic representative of its catchment population's interests, and had housed its activities. These are now largely excluded in favour of outside bodies and rent-paying activities. Comparison between this LVO's present and past thus shows this to be an example of organisational diversion. It is placed in the *divergent* category.

19. The *Residents* meet broad objectives of representing the interests of people in the area and also have some influence on the ethos of the community. Its interests are varied but its clientèle is geographically defined. It is therefore *generalist* though *inward-looking*; it has *no paid staff*. Its structure is *democratic* and it appears to have reached maturity, with its activities on a well-established plateau. It is thus *static*.

20. The *S Wales WEA Branch* is *generalist* in its interests, *inward-looking*, has *no staff* and is *democratic*. There is no evidence of significant departure from the group's firm resistance to opportunities of active study or to create additional facilities for others who might wish to do so. The governing group see themselves as upholding and perpetuating a great tradition, and it would appear that this LVO is *static*, though its members' own comparisons with their memories of the group's past as they see it suggests decline into the *divergent* category.

21. *The Kelvedon WEA* is *generalist*, *inward-looking*, has *no staff* and is *democratic*. It appears to be on a *static* plateau of very substantial group activity. However, current organisational developments involve the possibility of the group undertaking some new commitments and suggest that it may be moving into a dynamic phase.

22. *Wildlife* is *specialist* and *inward-looking* in its main objectives although there are generalist by-products. There is *no staff* and it is *democratic*. It has a substantial range of activities and links with other organisations and engages successfully in advocacy as well as practical and educational activities in its field. As a group it appears to be mainly *static* at present but seems to have dynamic tendencies.

23. *The Writers* are *specialist*, *inward-looking*, have *no staff*, and are *democratic*. As individual members of the group they show evidence of considerable development and personal change but the group as such,

though very active indeed, appears to be *static*.

24. The Gardeners are *specialist*, *inward-looking*, have *no staff*, and are *democratic*. The group's structure, activities and modes of operation have been established for generations and proved successful. It is effectively mature and as such largely *static*.

25. The *Pigeon Fanciers* are *specialist*, *inward-looking*, have *no staff*, are *democratic*. Purposes and activities have been long established and cannot be altered without bringing the group into conflict with its national organisation and thus frustrating its raison d'être. It is effectively mature and *static* as such.

26. The *PTA* serves a *specialist* purpose, is *inward-looking*, has *no paid staff* and is *democratic*. It appears to experience difficulty in involving parents other than members of its committee in anything it arranges. Parent committee members are active, but since there is currently no membership at large the group is best described as *static* with *divergent* tendencies.

27. The *Playgroup* meets the needs of a limited clientèle and is therefore *specialist* and *inward-looking*. It has a *democratic* structure, and employs *paid staff* as well as exploiting its substantial volunteer rota. It has learned how to manage its staff and is now engaged in penetrating the village establishment and involving more people in supporting it. It is therefore *dynamic*.

28. *Volunteer Drivers* are *specialist*, *outward-looking* because employed in meeting the needs of elderly and sick people who use their services. The organisation is supported by *paid staff*; it is *not democratic* because it is managed for them by another organisation. It is currently *static*.

29. *Aekta SH*, as a self-help group for Asian carers, is *specialist* and *inward-looking*. In its initial stages it is still being substantially supported by paid professional staff seconded to but not employed by it. It is thus only *incipiently democratic*, on its initial group learning and developmental curve and thus *dynamic*.

30. *Mountain Rescue* is *specialist* but solely *outward-looking*, has *no staff* of its own, and is *democratic*. A paradoxical feature of its *dynamic* stance is that the group's structure, functions and external relationships all force upon it a need to continually absorb new knowledge and technique in order to maintain its efficiency: it has to be dynamic in order to remain static.

31. *UIMWO* is *generalist*, *outward-looking*, *substantially staffed*, has a *democratic* constitution and is recorded accordingly. However, since there is no local membership in the normal sense of the word the committee cannot be very representative. In practice the organisation appears staff-governed as well as staff-run, and staff are engaged in delivering social and

welfare activity under contract to the public services. Having been largely diverted from its original objectives (which are comparable to those of the Settlement) it is in the *divergent* category.

The foregoing information is summarised, though in a different form and with additional detail not here under discussion, in the table on p. 131 below.

What Do the Categories Suggest?

Taking the obvious generalities first, it comes as no surprise that staffing features mainly with outward-looking generalist groups, and few inward-looking specialists have any. Most of the specialist groups, too, are inward-looking. What is more surprising is that all three groups which are firmly in the divergent category have paid staff, and they are outward-looking and social or welfare-oriented. The three static ones with strongly divergent tendencies have no paid staff, but two of the three are provided with continuous and substantial professional backing and advice from other sources.

Such small numbers cannot be interpreted as meaning that possession of professional staff is an obstacle to organisational learning and development. However, they suggest that professional staff may not always exert a constructive influence. In Chapter 3 (p. 35f. above) the more substantial Retford evidence suggested the same connection and linked it to centralised philanthropic organisations, weak or non-existent democracy and staff who are members of a hierarchy which is not appointed by or responsible to the local group.

Correlating the dynamic and static columns with other results does not produce any clear outcomes, and the small numbers introduce additional uncertainty. There appears, for instance, to be no relationship between the degree of individual member commitment exhibited by LVOs and whether they belong in the dynamic or static columns. This agrees with the argument presented earlier that, except where a static group exhibits regressive symptoms, stasis represents a different but no less constructive status than dynamism.

All these findings are, of course, based upon the illustrative but not representative sample of 31 case studies. The important differences between this and the more representative Retford sample were explained in Chapter 3. It was noted there that the case study sample reflects the decision, after satisfying the necessary criteria, to pick successful organisations wherever possible. Consequently the distribution of dynamic, static and divergent organisations differs between the main and Retford samples. If those static organisations which have marked regressive tendencies are transferred to the divergent category, the following table of distribution percentages emerges:

Diagram 15: Stance of organisations – case studies and Retford (%)

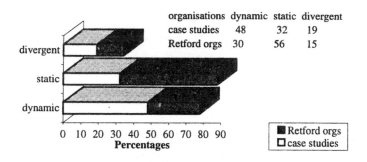

organisations	dynamic	static	divergent
case studies	48	32	19
Retford orgs	30	56	15

However, if we simply distinguish between those which are in good heart and those which are not, then the differences between samples dwindle into insignificance. Staffing, size, funding and objectives relate to each other in the same way, confirming, as was shown in Reynolds *et al.* (p. 33), that it is relatively large scale welfare work which requires staff and attracts funding, with everything else following upon that nexus, rather than the other way round. What is significant, however, is that in the Retford sample, as in the case studies, long-established philanthropic organisations again provide a distinct majority both of the divergent category and of static groups tending towards divergence. The distribution of inward- and outward-looking organisations and specialist and generalist ones does not differ sufficiently between the two samples to signify anything remarkable. It may therefore be accepted that the representative Retford sample broadly confirms conclusions drawn from the 31 about the causes of organisational learning and change.

What Are the Possible Causes?

Internal: Objectives and organisational patterns

The first question to consider here is whether objectives play any part in shaping an LVO's learning or developmental stance. Eleven of the sample organisations had outward-looking objectives and 20 were inward-looking. The sample included no organisation which was solely sociable although an ostensibly outward group – the Rotary Club – had been diverted to become mainly sociable and therefore primarily inward. However, it is notable that of the six groups which had been diverted or showed strong divergent tendencies, five had staff of their own or attached to them and none of these staff members was functionally under the control of members' representatives, whatever the theory of their employment. All these five were social service or welfare-oriented. Moreover, in two of the three definite divergents there was no sign of active democracy or membership responsibility and in the third it was known that it had never existed. Judging by the case study sample it may therefore be possible that there could be links between the availability of staff in somewhat directive roles, absence of functioning democracy, and social and welfare objectives.

The Retford sample strongly confirms the link between philanthropic objectives and either weak or absent democracy, though a link with possession of staff is less clear. Nevertheless, the comparison allows us to conclude that organisations whose objectives are welfare-oriented, which have no functioning democratic base, and which may have handed over effective control to paid professionals, are liable to regress and stop learning, changing and adapting. This links directly with the findings of the Volunteer Centre (1991) and Knight (1993) about difficulty in recruiting volunteers, and our Retford finding that these organisations tended to be isolationist, standing apart from the close-knit co-operative networks in the town.

Apart from three groups with strongly regressive tendencies all those which fall into the static category succeed (some admirably so) in meeting their objectives. It has already been pointed out that for certain kinds of organisations stasis is a, and possibly *the*, natural and desirable goal. Thus individual Gardeners continue to learn and develop, though the society itself has ceased to change, its size determined by the available land. Any imaginable dynamism would seem to promise only disadvantages, and be therefore a form of regression.

Interestingly, of all the groups with static characteristics only three (the Guildhouse, the Volunteer Drivers and the normally dynamic Arts Centre with its temporary and partial stasis) are outward-looking. It should be noted, too, that the majority of the Arts Centre's membership has inward objectives and specialist tastes. There is also a slightly lower but still substantial degree of correlation between stasis and specialist orientation. This looks like chance, and it may be that the high concentration of specialist groups in this category is responsible for the virtual absence of employed staff. The only exceptions are the Volunteer Drivers and the Guildhouse, where only office staff are directly employed and (marginally) the Arts Centre which, with new staff, was resuming its normal dynamism.

A fairly clear picture of causation has emerged of divergent and static groups. When the dynamic organisations are compared with each other the pattern seems at first obscure. At seven and eight respectively, generalist and specialist organisations are equally represented. With such small numbers six outward- and nine inward-looking ones are not far apart. The numbers with and without staff are also close together. However, a pattern does emerge when further comparisons are made, and two characteristics are clearly significant. Firstly, all but one of the dynamic organisations have effectively functioning representative democratic structures, and the apparently authoritarian exception (Fifty-Plus) is, in reality, exceedingly informal. Secondly, 13 of the 15 involve their members in a high or exceptionally high degree of personal participative commitment. The two exceptions may well be due to a mixture of cultural factors and newness of the organisation. Moreover, it may be significant that in most dynamic groups with paid staff the relationship between staff and members was very close and informal, and in all of them staff members were under the direct authority of members' representative governing bodies. Comparison with the Retford sample again shows close similarities in all respects.

It appears, then, that certain factors concerned with group objectives and internal structure tend towards dynamism, stasis or regression in organisations:

- Social- and social welfare-oriented LVOs, or others which, from different overt objectives, are moving strongly towards social ones, are at risk of regressing into divergence if they lack a strong internal democracy and employ or are supported by paid staff who accept or exploit weak member responsibility, rather than working to change it.
- Specialist inward-looking organisations, especially if not working in conjunction with professional staff, are likely to become static when they have reached a plateau of effective performance. For most, though not all, this is appropriate; except where a static group exhibits regressive symptoms, stasis represents maturity, a different but no less constructive stance than dynamism.
- Organisations which are effective democracies and elicit a high degree of active participation and commitment from their members, are likely to maintain a dynamic learning and developmental stance. If they have paid staff these will be responsible to the membership through its committees, and have recruitment and support of volunteers among their functions.
- A generalist group has to continually develop new projects or activities to remain dynamic (e.g. Ingleton CA, the WI Group, Bassetlaw CVS). If it ceases it will become static (e.g. Guildhouse) and may become divergent (e.g. Ujima, W London CA, S Wales WEA, UIMWO).
- A specialist group is less tied because less complex. It can be dynamic or, once it has reached full effectiveness, it can successfully occupy a static plateau. Only if it allows its standards to slip will it regress into divergence.

Internal: The influence of individuals

Here, again, the testimony of independent observers was of particular importance. That of staff members was carefully taken into account, while bearing in mind that it could not be regarded as independent. The preceding section has revealed some aspects of the negative influence paid staff may have on group learning and development where structure, arrangements and relationships arising from them are unfavourable. Ways of avoiding such problems are discussed in Chapter 9. It is at least possible, however, that leading members may affect group learning, regardless of whether or not there is a paid staff. It will also be necessary to look into any distinctions there may be between relationships which are structurally determined and those which are informal and due to personal qualities. There are thus two groups of individuals of whom some account should be given at this stage: paid staff, and members who showed particular leadership or innovatory qualities.

Paid Staff

A total of 68 staff members were employed in 13 of the main sample of 31 LVOs. Many of these were supposedly part-time but in effect worked far longer hours. We therefore did not distinguish between full- and part-time appointments. Of the total, 28 worked in small (fewer than 30 members) organisations, two in medium (30–99) and 38 in large ones. We classified staffs relatively as small, medium and large in proportion to the size and complexity of their employing organisations. This resulted in a distribution of 16 to small staffs and 52 employed in medium to large ones. Nearly a third of the total were employed by a single organisation, UIMWO. Only one staff member was being paid from the internal funds of the employing organisation, and that payment was an honorarium of no more than £100 p.a.

The distribution of staff according to organisational objectives was much as expected. The following contrasted pairs (which do not necessarily add up to the total of 68) show staff members to be very strongly concentrated in generalist and outward-looking organisations, while even in the third pair the service-giving groups still had more than twice as many employees as those which are interest-based:

Diagram 16: Distribution of staff by objectives (N=68)

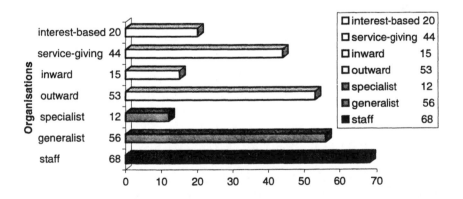

Sixty-six were employed in democratic organisations, but in a few instances, including the largest employer, that democracy seemed to be less than flourishing.

Finally there were two highly significant discoveries: just 34 of the 68 staff appeared to be very active learners in most or all the categories used in Chapter 5; and only five met the criteria we had set for identifying leaders and innovators among the members. These figures contrast with those for volunteer leaders below.

Leaders and Innovators

Virtually every LVO had its elected officers and committee. Our intention here was to identify those individuals among the respondents whose activities were shaping or changing the course of their LVOs, or had done so in the past. There were 51 of them (and no doubt others among the many members who were not interviewed), just under 10% of those who were interviewed, and they came from a wide spread of 24 organisations. We found none among the respondents from seven LVOs, including three defined as divergent or nearly so. Not surprisingly all but 13 held elected offices. There were significantly more in inward-looking than outward-looking organisations but almost equal proportions in specialist and generalist ones. As one would expect, organisations without paid staff, small or medium organisations and those with slight or no funding threw up more leaders and innovators than their opposites.

Leaders and innovators were identified by reference solely to those criteria which are directly relevant to these roles. A comparison with the sample as a whole of this group's personal characteristics and also their learning and participatory behaviour is interesting. Those who had been most privileged educationally are the most prominent:

Diagram 17: TEA of leaders and main sample compared (%)

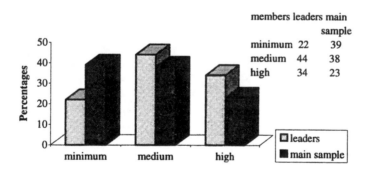

	members leaders	main sample
minimum	22	39
medium	44	38
high	34	23

The high TEA individuals are also more active and one and a half times as many as of the membership at large are members of other organisations as well. *All of them* are among the most active and committed learners. This finding is consistent at a highly significant level across all five categories of learning, and all LVOs, though most marked in the political, personal and organisational areas. The contrast to paid staff is marked.

It may be useful to consider staff and other influences upon group learning and development in relation to our established categories.

The Dynamic Group

Ingleton CA presents the most complex structure of all the case study organisations because it is an LVO whose range of activities includes provision from the County and District Councils, and its own daughter organisations, in addition to its direct provision. It has a strong group of highly creative elected leaders who are anxious to see maximum usage and development. The warden, on the other hand, is responsible to the organisation but also organises the LEA-provided formal class programme and supervises premises and ancillary staff on behalf of the statutory authority, as well as representing all parties in the management of the premises.

This is a structure which requires a maximum of warmth, generosity, imaginative flexibility and informed commonsense from both leading members and staff. Where this is forthcoming it is the group as a whole which gains and learns because the experience is assimilated to its total historical stock. If such characteristics were lacking in any of the leading individuals this could easily lead to open warfare, to under-use of premises, and to reduced income, especially in the current plight of general adult education, and consequently to reduced dynamism.

Chapter 5 set out the effects which the dynamism of the WI Group produces and transmits into every other organisation and aspect of village life. The case study records (cf. Stewart *et al.*, 1992) how the current practice of dispersal of responsibility, with its consequent rise in activity and influence, started from a rebellion against a long-term autocratic president under whose rule the Institute had become little more than her attenuated shadow. During the case study it was clear that the then current officers and committee members were effective democratic leaders. The interviews showed that past and future office holders, and even some of those few who had escaped it altogether were no less influential.

As in the case of the "Sibsey effect" (cf. pp. 62–65 above) on personal learning and change, neither TEA nor any social measure seemed to correlate with this level of group learning and development. Sibsey thus poses another riddle, and this time without clues to an answer: how can such a very representative and chance collection of women embrace so few who do *not* show leadership characteristics? And how do they succeed in pursuing all their activities creatively in friendship and co-operation untroubled by ambition? Is leadership quality far more common than is realised, but needs special conditions to be brought into the open? Do these include the typically nurturing and non-competitive attitudes of at any rate some female groups? The WI Group is possibly the most dynamic of the sample organisations, and throws up so much leadership quality without explaining itself that there is relatively little that can be learned from it in this particular respect, however instructive it is in others. Are there nevertheless parallels here with the almost all-male Mountain Rescue Team where the same attitudes, and the same potentially universal leadership were found? And are the answers, after all, the same as in the case of the "Sibsey effect"? The evidence is too limited for positive claims, but the questions it poses almost compel a series of affirmatives.

Bassetlaw CVS, though structurally more complex, offers clearer lessons on the effects of staff. The functions of this organisation can be roughly divided into three areas. One is interpretative – to make the community and its organisations aware of themselves and each other, to act as an honest broker between statutory authority and the voluntary sector in general, and to convert public finance into resources of manpower, skill, or material for LVOs through grants and the provision of education, training and organisational services. Another function is to act as the community's antennae, sensing where there might be unmet needs for action or services, and to stimulate action or organisation to meet them. A third is pioneering of new activities and services by direct intervention.

Bassetlaw CVS turned out to be dynamic in all these respects, continually learning and developing in its own right and assisting other LVOs to do so. The case study reveals two sets of reasons for this. One is the carefully representative structure of the organisation itself, which gives it direct personal links into the public services and the political structures of the community as well as the spectrum of voluntary organisations. The other seems to be rooted in the way in which staff operate, combining the role of dispensers of resources and services with personal ability. They make themselves and their resources available as enablers at the disposal of other organisations, pointing them tactfully in the right direction, helping them to discover their own potential and their strength and supporting rather than leading them in action. There is here a kind of "negative capability" which allows others as well as itself to grow to full stature.

Similar patterns of leadership seem to be responsible for the dynamism of several of the specialist organisations which do not employ staff. At Arthritis SH one individual with modest prior experience of responsibility through committee service took a determined lead with organisational support from the CVS and its Self-Help Network. At the Railway Trust it was individual enthusiasts who coalesced into a leading group. These were, and continue to be, prepared to give endless time and energy to their commitment and thus set an example which drew a very large number of others into their slipstream; these, in their turn, threw up new leadership potential by the same mechanism. At Fifty-Plus it was, again, individual leaders who not only had the necessary skills but were prepared to set an example of commitment which drew in others to assist them.

The Singers and the Settlement present more complex patterns, because in both the roles of paid and voluntary leadership are mingled; professionalism and volunteering are represented in the same individuals. At the Settlement staff wear their authority so lightly that they behave like volunteers for much of the time. As a result their authority may, in practice, derive more from the example of commitment than from their formal position. Consequently they elicit from their membership and from other paid staff a level of committed voluntary service which sometimes equates the two.

Among the Singers formal authority is vested in an elected committee of which the conductor is a member, but most members are such strong characters that the energy which drives the organisation has many sources. It is focused, however, in the administrative leadership of the secretary on the one hand and the musical authority of the conductor on the other. Nevertheless the relationship between conductor and group is reciprocal and egalitarian, with him setting ever more demanding goals and the membership as it were almost driving him to keep them at the very edge of their capacity. This kind of mutuality is perhaps partly comparable to that other continuously dynamic organisation, the Mountain Rescue Team, where all are leaders and all are led.

Some conclusions about the part played by individuals in stimulating group learning are possible from this brief survey. One is that personality is important but possibly not quite in the way that might sometimes be expected. Among this dynamic group, at any rate, all or most are willing to take on substantial responsibility and work persistently at it, but none of the leading individuals are what might be called "commanding figures". What they have in common is ability indeed, but it is deployed to discover interests, needs and potential in themselves, and to enable others to identify and pursue their own goals. It displays willingness to take risks and set an example of intense commitment, which supports others in following that example. High levels of individual learning and change seem to be inseparable from dynamism of groups, but the most successful of the dynamic groups are distinguished by leadership which acts in or through groups rather than individualistically.

The Static Group

Organisations which do not employ staff exhibit a similar pattern to most of the dynamic group. All include obvious leading individuals who mostly continue in that role for long periods, especially if they have been founder members. In some instances as they age they are replaced in active leadership tasks by younger individuals, but remain in formal or informal but less demanding roles. The NWR Group, though dynamic in the programme context, has some static characteristics as well. Without formal structure of any kind, nevertheless it includes individuals who have informal leadership roles in so far as they are regular sources of good ideas, may be good at making contacts or consistently advocate thoughtful topics and display skill at guiding discussion unobtrusively in constructive directions. In this group it seems possible to distinguish more clearly perhaps than elsewhere the kind of leading individuals whose talent tends towards dynamism and those who have more of a maintenance role.

In those groups which had attained a plateau of effective stability this could, as at Kelvedon WEA and with the Widows SH, involve a change in the kind of leadership given by certain individuals. These had obviously had a dynamic role in an earlier phase. As the organisation reached the phase of continuous and stable activity they either adapted to more managerial functions or withdrew into formal roles – or went on to higher office elsewhere.

Both the Guildhouse and the Arts Centre (which is now dynamic again but discussed here because of a passing static phase) owe their initial development to exceptional individuals in the great tradition of liberal adult education, i.e. people who were professionals in the sense in which the term could be used of staff at the Settlement. They were totally committed to their caring and shaping and teaching task, and exceptionally skilled at it. The founder of the Arts Centre (the warden of the neighbouring adult education centre) was, in addition, a distinguished and successful trainer. The personal stamp of an outstanding leader remains on organisations not because they are remembered; they are remembered because many others – both volunteers and professionals – have learned their trade from their example and continue to perpetuate it in the group learning of these centres.

However, the fate of the two institutions differs. The Guildhouse is now directed by elderly volunteers who follow the example of their early mentor's personal dedication but lack the professional equipment and time needed to interpret that lesson in modern curricular and organisational terms. As a result organisational learning was confined to the process of learning to make do without a warden, and then ceased.

The Arts Centre, on the other hand, acquired specialised professional staffing of its own while keeping the tradition of dedicated and highly skilled voluntary leadership. Its problem has been that its finances only permit it to appoint young and inexperienced staff who have to learn the skills of working with volunteers as well as their more specific responsibilities, and who understandably tend to leave soon for better paid posts. This places greater than usual demands upon the voluntary leadership in maintaining group learning and development. Their role includes tasks such as 'holding the fort' and settling in new staff. The centre is fundamentally dynamic but has temporary static features because at the time of the case study a new staff team was – albeit quickly and enthusiastically – finding its feet. Nevertheless, the Arts Centre case study no less than the Settlement and the Singers provided us with some of the most valuable detailed evidence on constructive co-operation between paid professional manpower and volunteers, and this will be further explored in Chapters 8 and 9 below.

The Divergent Group

Just as there are obviously dynamic leaders in the group of dynamic organisations and some others good at maintenance in the static, so some of the divergent or near-regressive groups throw up people in leadership roles who reinforce such trends. Examples are the warden (he had significantly adopted the title "director") of the W London CA, whose policy centres on profitability and security. He has had the CA's constitution adapted to create a "board of directors" which backs this kind of leadership. At the S Wales WEA Branch it was the committee under its powerful long-term chairman which firmly resisted any change or expansion in Branch activity. UIMWO was concentrating its efforts on the pursuit of contracts and other remunerated service activities under leadership which seemed focused on financial and managerial roles. These absorbed energies which, in former times, might have been devoted to local membership and community development activities.

Both in the sample organisations and those at Retford the kinds of leadership roles (staff or member) which seemed to predominate in such problematic groups tended to be authoritarian and sometimes manipulative. They were complemented and indeed favoured (perhaps partly caused) by the absence or weakness of democratic structures in the groups concerned.

On the other hand there were exceptions to this kind of leadership in these organisations. In Rotary two members with leadership roles continued to give priority to social service functions. One of these, perhaps not fully satisfied with opportunities provided by the club, was serving as a volunteer literacy tutor in a personal capacity but as a result of experience with the club. Another exception was the PTA, where an officer single-handedly transformed objectives from mere money-raising to a primary educational emphasis.

Such personal instances cannot be said to exemplify group learning. Leadership as such will be discussed in more detail in relation to the topic of processes and outcomes, in Chapter 9. The evidence about the impact of individuals on group learning and development is very substantial, and only a selection of it has been presented here. Some of its more obvious aspects may be summarised at this stage:

- Leaders and staff of really exceptional quality are inevitably uncommon. However, the kind of voluntary or paid leadership which results in groups learning and developing effectively on a continuing basis occurs quite often, but not regularly. Chance plays a part, but it seems most likely to surface where conditions are difficult and much commitment is required, and where relationships are mutually caring, egalitarian and democratic.

- Groups seem to learn and develop best where the leadership (including paid staff) is non-competitive, continually involves other members and disperses real responsibility among them as much as possible. Effective training and nurturing of a succession of new leaders is in itself a way of securing the group's continuing flexibility and responsiveness.

External Causes of Group Learning and Change: The influence of the statutory sector

In this section, more perhaps than some others, we are able to reinforce the intensive case study sample with the findings from the extensive one at Retford. This justifies some confident interim statements:

- No voluntary organisation can learn, change or develop unless it survives, and some LVOs cannot survive without substantial support, sometimes in more than one form, from public sources. The most obvious examples of this are those which perform some kind of welfare or major cultural function with members who are unable to meet the cost of what is being provided, or where the cost would exclude the majority. Others need more limited assistance and a further group are aided by some authorities because they are thought to make a constructive contribution without which the quality of a community's life would be diminished. In some instances as little as some simple moral support and public countenance can be valuable to an organisation.

None of our three data bases furnished us with a reliable measure of the proportions of LVOs which receive different kinds of support or training from public sources. Retford information is biased in this respect because the Bassetlaw District is one of the most generous (within the resources at its disposal) and far-sighted in the country in its support of voluntary activity in the local community (Association of District Councils, 1992). The main data base is less biased in this regard, but does include the group of Nottinghamshire LVOs. Moreover, the sampling process, it will be recalled, picked successful organisations wherever a choice was available. The numbers of organisations in any of the categories which follow are therefore not necessarily an accurate representation of national distribution, but the conclusions about relationships rest on solid evidence.

Seventeen of the 31 sample organisations (an inflated figure as has been stated) depend on the public sector in some way or other for their very existence. This may be through the provision of grant, accommodation of their own or the use of public premises, ad hoc services or assistance, the training of personnel, and combinations of all or any of these. It includes the symbiosis which enables the District Council's Leisure and Tourism Department and the Railway Trust to benefit each other, or the rather less equal relationship between the Fifty-Plus Group, which needs the local leisure centre and that centre's grudging co-operation with users whose presence is essential to its own survival. It includes provision of staff as at Ingleton CA and the W London CA, grant aid which could be a small but valuable extra as for the S Wales WEA, or core finance, as at Bassetlaw CVS.

Core finance, in turn, can vary widely. For Bassetlaw CVS it is sufficient to give the organisation a secure foundation to which other sources can be attracted. Lower levels may impose damaging limitations but still enable the organisation to plan with some degree of security as at the Arts Centre. Alternatively core finance, as at the Settlement, may be too small and insecure to create an adequate foundation and this may, as at UIMWO, cause the virtual corruption of an organisation's objectives by means of excessive reliance upon short-term funding by contract finance, which distorts both staffing and activity. We are aware of fortunate and exceptional examples of LVOs of this kind, whose endowments suffice to produce a core income which pays essential salaries and provides and maintains accommodation, but they are few.

Core finance is thus a prime condition of organisational development for organisations which need external help. By far the most productive way the project observed for the delivery of core finance from public sources was the relationship which created a supportive network between the County and District Authorities in Bassetlaw, the Bassetlaw CVS (including the Self Help Network) and the huge body of LVOs. The CVS is itself an independent LVO. As such it provides the public sector with an arms-length channel for grant aid, and with skilled professionals to assess requirements, distribute grant or help in kind.

By means of the relationships which the CVS creates and the training it provides, the CVS and the statutory authorities ensure the current and future quality and development of work in the voluntary sector. Thus an LVO – perhaps a self-help group – would be founded on the initiative of one or more individuals, supported by relevant professionals, provided with accommodation, a start-up grant, office services and publicity, and supportive training for the leaders of the new organisation. As they gain confidence, professional support is withdrawn and redeployed elsewhere. On rare occasions, where professionals discern the need for a particular kind of self-help group first, they may reverse the process by finding suitable founder members, as in the case of Aekta SH.

Given the money or other resources without which some organisations cannot come into existence or survive, constructive supervision and training, however informal, are the next most important contribution the statutory sector can make to ensure learning and positive development of LVOs. The lack of this element, together with funding beyond the capacity of inexperienced people to administer appropriately, caused the collapse of Ujima. Constructive supervision does not necessarily require a professional and arms-length body like Bassetlaw CVS. County Social Services provided it direct for the Volunteer Drivers and by a necessarily generous but presumably temporary staff secondment to Aekta SH, while the police force, the health service and the Royal Air Force all contribute relevant skills to the regular inservice training of the Mountain Rescue Team.

Some organisations only need free or cheap use of publicly provided premises to become or remain dynamic or at least healthily static. The partial or complete disappearance of this facility in many parts of the country owing to local management of schools and the drying up of grants to village halls and community centres has had a literally devastating effect on very many LVOs, as has the abandonment of affiliation schemes excepting some for voluntary youth clubs. In some areas these may still receive grant aid, loans of camping equipment and the like, and occasional coaching.

Civic recognition without any material benefit can play a notable part in developing an organisation's learning as well as its impact (as in the case of the Singers) and may greatly expand its opportunities for responsibility, learning and development as at Sibsey or Ingleton or, in the past, at the Guildhouse. Organisations such as these, or almost all the daughter organisations of Ingleton CA or the lodgers of the W London CA, receive nothing or next to nothing from public sources except perhaps listing in a record of local activities. They probably constitute a very large majority of LVOs.

Relations with the public sector are thus very variable. The large Retford sample shows that even in this special area the majority of LVOs have none and do not need any. This was found to be especially the case with organisations which were specialist, or inward-looking, or small, or had no staff. The reasons are simple: specialist and inward-looking groups (whether darts clubs or archaeological societies) are least likely to need outside resources; small groups are unlikely to have paid staff, who usually require subsidy except in near-commercial ventures such as a golf club or professional football. Paid staff usually make learning and organisational links in addition to financial ones because they have the time and realise the potential. The links are likely to be strongest in the social and welfare area because here the need for subsidy is greatest.

The quality of statutory influence upon LVOs depends on whether public authorities wish to respect and foster the voluntary contribution, or follow current government policy by turning voluntary organisations into cheap substitutes for statutory social, health and welfare, and educational services. Where there is an intelligent and constructive policy as in the one area where we were able to trace its full extent, the public sector is able to ensure that work best done by the voluntary sector is done well. It also contributes deliberately through co-operation and training (sometimes delegated as at Retford) with a wide range of LVOs, to their effectiveness in their own terms and their ability to improve their contribution to the community's quality of life.

The LVOs, in their turn, provide a training ground in active citizenship for their members. This reinforces civil society locally and strengthens the base of local political leadership. Local councillors emerge from the LVO sector and local officials are kept well informed of needs, opinion and potential. Group learning here is not a one-way process; the public sector, where it is wise, "realises the value of voluntary expertise, energy, information, suggestions, and critique" (Reynolds *et al.*, 1994). Thus group learning becomes reciprocal and the relationship symbiotic.

External Influences: Networking

Much group learning results from the close interaction which was found to exist among voluntary organisations and between them, the statutory sector and also local business and industry, and the professions. Independent evidence was particularly strong in this area. One of our interim papers (Elsdon, 1995) points to the evidence from the Retford study that "voluntary organisations are not isolated or solitary creatures, and the voluntary sector does not exist in a different universe from the public sector or, for that matter, from business, industry and professional services. They inhabit a single world, serve and above all consist of the same people who breathe the same air and walk the same streets. All of them interact, their personnel overlaps, and all depend on each other in various ways."

That mutual group learning takes place through this whole network of organisations, and that it is substantial, was shown in our Retford study in particular (Reynolds *et al.*, 1994), where its high level of incidence could be shown statistically and its pathways were illustrated by means of diagrams based on actual LVOs and individuals. It is more difficult to illustrate the process qualitatively except in certain instances and especially where substantial umbrella bodies such as Bassetlaw CVS are involved (cf. p. 112f. above).

At Ingleton CA, for instance, mutual learning ensured, in the first instance, that daughter organisations were taught more efficient organisational and financial practices, and long-term planning of resource development. This led them to raise their standards continuously. Some of the daughter LVOs in their turn gradually caused the umbrella organisation to adopt more liberal attitudes especially towards young people, to broaden its concerns beyond the immediate locality, and to take on board a concern for economic development.

At the Arts Centre there was evidence that local dramatic societies could learn and adopt higher standards from each other and, particularly, as a result of the centre's influence and that of visiting professionals. There was also interplay between taught and amateur groups in the visual arts and crafts, between all these and academic study in the arts at the partnering adult education centre, and there had been similar mutual benefits between those two and the LEA's music centre until this became a victim of the government's reorganisation of further education.

More informal mutual learning between different groups has been described in the case of the Singers, where there is evidence, also, of influence on local authority cultural policy at home and abroad, and on business groups. The Writers draw much of their social and political energy from their umbrella organisation, and are contributing their experience of creative but informal group work to others like themselves. Fifty-Plus provides evidence of social and health services' policies being affected substantially. The testimony of outside observers of the Settlement shows how powerfully this affects other groups. At the same time both it and its daughter organisations are learning to maintain their identities, adapt to changing social conditions and above all to the organisational and financial problems caused by ever-changing but always short-term government policies and their sometimes eccentric local applications.

More individual instances of group learning by co-operation or networking are so numerous that a few examples must suffice. The Playgroup is learning political skills while teaching the local village hall committee to accept broader objectives. The Gardeners are reaching for an understanding not just of their own needs and others' who have lost their jobs, but those, for example, of old age through their generous link with the local old people's home. Wildlife and the Archaeologists are using their local WEA Districts and University extramural departments to train new members and broaden and deepen the groups' expertise. Fifty-Plus provides volunteers and organisational skills for several social welfare organisations for old people – the list could continue to include developmental interaction of churches and their own daughter organisations and other LVOs, between youth service, sporting and church bodies, between public houses, sport and charitable bodies, and many others.

The effect is, as it were, confirmed by a few instances where group learning seemed to be deliberately resisted. This has been mentioned in the case of the S Wales WEA Branch. It appeared to be a possible motive behind the new constitutional arrangements of the W London CA.

Conclusion

That groups do learn and acquire – or lose – developmental momentum or, in a few instances, actually regress either deliberately to satisfy external or internal vested interests, or owing to external changes, chance and often personal factors, can now be regarded as established. Some of the detailed evidence has been summarised at intervals throughout this chapter. It remains to be seen whether a return to the categorisation at the beginning of this chapter yields further illumination.

Beginning with the divergent group and the three LVOs with strong divergent tendencies, it appears that none of these six organisations has yielded instances of group (as distinct from individual) learning. Three or possibly four of the static group seemed similarly inactive unless the Pigeon Fanciers' permanent preoccupation with the invention and prevention of foul play is to count as group learning. All those categorised as dynamic and at least half the static provided strong and numerous instances of group learning. If we now return to the findings of Chapter 5 and apply its categories to the incidence of group learning and change, it appears that a very similar distribution emerges. The only notable difference is that two LVOs which demand from their individual members very great individual commitment and learning (Gardeners and Pigeon Fanciers) appear among the static mature group and do little if any *group* learning or networking. Apart from this, if the sources of evidence are meshed, several strong conclusions emerge:

- High levels of individual learning and development, and of group learning and development, go together with an organisation's commitment to learning and social or caring objectives. They produce dynamic development on the part of that organisation unless it is one that has matured and only requires the maintenance of its efficiency.

- The evidence of group learning across networks which may include the public as well as the economic and professional sectors shows that group, like individual learning and development, is transmitted.

- This transmission has no inbuilt geographical limits. It is naturally commonest where there is direct and frequent local contact. However, evidence – some of it substantial – shows that the learning and experience of a group can spark off or greatly influence other groups and individuals anywhere in the country, occasionally abroad and – with chance connections – in some eccentrically remote spots.

Chapter 8

Are Communities Affected by LVOs?

The immediately preceding chapters have taken this account to, and through, the central part of our evidence. They have shown that individuals can and usually do learn, change and develop in a rich variety of ways when involved in membership of LVOs, and that the LVOs themselves are organisms which necessarily undergo analogous development. The purpose of this chapter is to demonstrate in some detail that organisations are no more "islands" than individuals. They function in and are part of local geographical and political communities; they rub shoulders with, relate to each other, form organisational networks with the public and possibly economic and professional sectors of a community's life, just as their individual members have roles in different organisations and form personal networks across them.

The Field Evidence

Readers of the intensive evidence contained in some of our case studies and of the extensive but inclusive findings of the Retford study (both sources amply reinforced by the testimony of independent observers) will think the interrogative chapter heading redundant. After all, 50% of outside observers volunteered views such as that LVOs helped to make the local public more aware of social concerns, and 41% had found them contributing to health and safety. Thirty-nine per cent pointed to gains in independent living due to LVO intervention and smaller numbers noted environmental and other benefits. The Retford study, especially, is full of examples and includes substantial uncommitted testimony. Some of this material will contribute to the concluding section of this chapter. However, if the question is to be justifiably turned into an assertion, then the intervening evidence and argument must rest upon more detailed evidence. This requires a final trawl through the case studies.

For this purpose the case studies are divided into two main groups and various sub-groups according to the kind of impact suggested by the evidence:

Kinds of Impact on Local Communities

Group A:
1. negative
2. neutral

Group B:
1. minor effects, those which are not easily perceptible, or those which are conveyed through individuals
2. through specific facilities and opportunities affecting the lives and

opportunities of individuals, groups and community
3.   through pervasive changes affecting the quality of life in the area, or notable aspects of it (*includes* 2. above)
4.   through effects on broadly or specifically political consciousness, activity, or structure of the area and the nature of its civil society.

It should be borne in mind throughout this chapter, including the tabulation which follows the analysis, that there is no intention here to construct a hierarchy. Obviously, organisations in Group A are judged to be less successful *in this particular respect* than those in Group B, but no such distinction obtains between the organisations or the sub-groups within Group B. They make different kinds and quantities of impact, by different means, on local society simply because they are different organisations, have different objectives, activities, and ways of conducting their affairs.

All those LVOs in the sample which were placed in the third sub-group of Group B above proved also to belong in the fourth. In consequence the two categories were amalgamated, both in the analytical paragraphs and the tabulation which follows them. The distinction is preserved, however, because in a different sample categories 3 and 4 might have differed more. The case studies are assigned to one of the sub-groups (more than one where appropriate) on the basis of the available evidence. The reader is reminded that in all instances the decision rests on independent testimony as well as evidence from within the LVO. Each example will be individually considered in order to discover the activities, structures or agencies by which the impact has been made, in one or more of the following ways:

Impact through:
1.   Particular individuals:
     either: (a) as overt and active leaders
     or: (b) as links or enablers
2.   Co-operative action:
     either: (a) internal
     or: (b) external
3.   Use or provision of an umbrella structure
4.   Support in or action on a network structure.

These categories will be illustrated in the descriptive paragraphs which follow, and the analytical table which summarises these (p. 131 below) will use the same classification by number and letter.

After this description and categorisation it will be practicable to investigate whether there are any links between an LVO's impact upon the community and its characteristics as an organisation. Finally, an attempt will be made to draw conclusions from the analysis as a whole.

A caveat must be entered before assigning each case study LVO to a group. The process is inevitably rough-and-ready because an LVO's impact is bound to be mixed; among our sample even those which appear to be negative or neutral are thought to have some positive effects. These may not have been displayed to the researchers or, if known, may have been outweighed by others when the table came to be constructed. In any case, listing and analysis are confined to characteristics which are relevant to the particular issue here under discussion. Bearing this in mind, there follows a descriptive analysis in which the LVOs are assigned to subgroups, and their relationship (if any) to the local community, and the activities or structures which bear that relationship, are described. The order of entries within each sub-group is not significant.

A. Negative and Neutral Effects

Ujima tried to provide advisory, counselling and some welfare services and education in citizenship for the local African-Caribbean and Asian population. Its leaders tried to run before they could walk. The LA gave the stumbling organisation an excessively powerful financial push, which, far from speeding its progress, made it fall flat on its face. Both the organisation's leaders and its link organisation (the LA) were thus agents of its downfall. Thus services which seemed, briefly, to be available to the public were not just lost; owing to the loss of confidence they will be all the more difficult to re-establish.

UIMWO has the reputation of having conducted important and successful community activities as well as welfare work in the past. From limited observation and interviews it appeared that, despite good intentions, most of what was observed tended to encourage dependency and deference in the small number of clients the team was enabled to see. The causes appeared to be multiple. An obvious one was the approach of community staff and their lack of contact with good practice. The organisation's own umbrella and networking functions had been largely overtaken by contractual and related activities. It carried out dedicated welfare activities of its own and tasks which, in different circumstances, would be undertaken by the public services. In terms of developing active citizenship its effect seemed to be negative.

The W London CA, by changing itself in the manner described in Chapter 7, has ceased to perform, in its own right, any tasks which could be described as being of service to the majority of its local community, though it provides organisations from elsewhere with accommodation. Its mode of action has, indeed, become a source of conflict with the local community and its representative organisation. The causes appear to be the policies initiated by paid staff, compounded by commercial policies which have been introduced by the LA on which this LVO depends. The organisation's impact on its local community must be regarded as negative.

The Rotary Club tries to be of service to its local area but its impact is so slight as to be rated neutral. It may be that lack of leadership from within and from the national umbrella body are among the reasons.

The South Wales WEA Branch provides a possibly useful outlet for a small group of elderly people, but its contribution to the community at large seems to be neutral. The reasons appear to be the refusal of the leader-ship to contemplate change, and the absence of links with comparable organisations, or of effective support from the umbrella body.

B. Positive Effects

1. MINOR, NOT EASILY PERCEPTIBLE, OR CONVEYED THROUGH INDIVIDUALS
The NWR Group's constitution prevents it, as an organisation, from tak-ing up a stance on public issues. However, through the actions which its educational activity prompts individuals to take, it influences the climate of opinion locally on particular issues. Examples include outside speak-ers such as the police officer who, as a result of discussion with the group, introduced new policies and physical facilities for women vic-tims. There is also evidence of effective pressure by members who se-cured changes at local schools. The causes of its external effects are to be found mainly in the degree of individual empowerment caused by a high level of internal co-operation. Despite the group's informality, there is some evidence of both overt and enabling leadership by individuals.

The Guildhouse (see also under 3/4 below) provides important facilities for the use of the public and presents an example of effective internal de-mocracy. Judged by the team's observation and other independent evi-dence, these characteristics currently exert some slight influence through relatively isolated individuals among its membership who occupy influ-ential positions elsewhere or who are connected to such individuals.

The Writers spread their political and cultural awareness and advocacy both by word of mouth and by publications which circulate modestly. Their own practice and organisation demonstrate their egalitarianism, and there is continual interchange with others both through their local umbrella body and the network of similar writers' groups which arose partly as a result of their influence.

The Allotment Society provides facilities which are important especially to elderly and unemployed individuals, and supplies resources and advice to members of the public. It probably has some influence as a successful long-term stable democratic organisation, but its specific impact is mod-est and probably confined to internal co-operation among members and perhaps some others who are made generously aware of old people's ex-istence and some simple means of assisting those in need. The society's rules are also exemplary in encouraging the prevention of mess and dis-order in public areas.

The Pigeon Fanciers are even more private than the allotment gardeners, but here, too, internal co-operation ensures an awareness of good neigh-bourly behaviour.

The Parent Teacher Association makes modest contributions to general awareness of parental responsibility towards and opportunities for support of schools, mainly through the activity of one individual member.

2. THROUGH SPECIFIC FACILITIES AND OPPORTUNITIES AFFECTING THE LIVES AND OPPORTUNITIES OF INDIVIDUALS, GROUPS AND COMMUNITY

It should be noted that all the organisations listed below this point provide, by definition, services and opportunities for all those members of the public who wish, or need, to avail themselves of them. Outline descriptions will be found in Chapter 3 and details in the case study volumes; the present tabulation concentrates on what organisations contribute beyond their core services.

The Widows' SH offers a counselling service and engages in substantial advocacy on behalf of widows. It educates the public in general and especially the staff of public services directly or indirectly concerned. It does this mainly because leading individual members have forged links with those in other organisations and, particularly, the public services and industry.

The Macular SH Group is a recent foundation. It serves the needs of those who are personally affected by the disease and their carers. It acts through a leading individual though some internal co-operation is beginning to develop. It still depends heavily on the skilled and generous support of an umbrella group (CVS) which is itself an LVO.

Patients' Support undertakes a task too sensitive for any kind of public knowledge to be allowed to emerge. However, its impact through individuals on their families and friends and through co-operation with an umbrella body, ensures that public awareness of and sympathy for those suffering from mental illness become stronger and better informed.

Arthritis SH is securing stronger public awareness of the plight of arthritis sufferers and of ways to assist them, such as improved access to shops and public buildings. The main agents of this impact are particular individuals, the group's growing co-operative efforts, and skilled and generous support by a CVS.

The Archaeological Society makes a co-operative impact on public knowledge and awareness through its programme of public lectures. Its influence is probably rather more effective through individual contacts and through public service by individual members, their participation in the planning process, and their public "whistleblowing" activities on behalf of the built and landscape heritage. They are assisted in these activities by networking with related LVOs and educational institutions locally and regionally.

The Singers exist, essentially, for the sake of their membership. Beyond this they introduce the public to a large repertoire of vocal music, and to good standards of performance. Other choirs and their conductors also benefit. This educational activity has been extended into a regular civic cultural and representational role, which, in turn, has spread the organisation's influence, both musically and as an example of a functioning autonomous democracy, through international exchanges. These, finally, have increased the members' and their families' and friends' interest in and understanding of international issues. The causes are complex and involved; they include overt and enabling leadership by different individuals, co-operation within the choir, with other musicians locally and abroad, with public authorities at home and abroad, and networking with a variety of musical, educational and charitable organisations.

Fifty-Plus makes provision for a very high proportion of its local target age group. For the community at large it makes the local leisure centre viable, keeps town centre vandalism at bay, and defends the local library against closure. It provides volunteer staffing for a number of social service activities aimed at less fit or fortunate old people than themselves, and acts as an effective example of voluntary service and active citizenship. According to medical and social services evidence it makes an important contribution to the physical and mental health of the community, acting both therapeutically and prophylactically. The agencies through which all this is delivered are both overt leaders and co-operative patterns within the organisation, which acts as an umbrella for a large number of activities. In addition it networks informally with outside service activities staffed by members, and with similar groups elsewhere, which it has founded or helps to develop.

The Railway Trust, in addition to its direct services, delivers substantial transferable training in organising, business and management skills to a high proportion of its members and trains many of them up in committee and officer skills. It makes a contribution of national significance to heritage and contributes to the local economy in partnership with the LA's tourism committee. Both overt and enabling leaders are active in this; there is strong internal co-operation. External co-operation with British Rail, relevant museums and LAs is mutually beneficial.

The Playgroup, beyond its immediate remit, provides parent education generally, including some fathers, and encourages the village hall committee to become more aware of responsibilities to the whole community. It makes its impact more particularly through enabling leadership and with assistance from its own umbrella body and the LA.

The Voluntary Car Scheme provides a basic service which enables the elderly and infirm to maintain independent activity and interests, and ensures by informal and personal means that a better understanding of their needs spreads among the population at large. It also assists in improving and maintaining the mental and physical health of some of the drivers. There is no formal agency of transmission; influence spreads by osmosis.

Aekta SH is too new to make any impact beyond itself, but it has led to better understanding between the Asian carers in its membership and some officers of the social services.

The Kelvedon Branch of the WEA, apart from its direct educational services, is continually training a cadre of skilled speakers, problem solvers, people who can discuss issues and discharge responsibility, for other groups in the village. It raises issues of civic importance and trains electors to assess evidence, debate it and make up their minds independently. This is achieved by direct leadership, by members playing enabling roles in other groups, by means of internal and external co-operation, by working with its own umbrella organisation and networking informally with others.

The Wildlife Trust provides environmental and heritage training and information, and advocacy (including political action where necessary); it cherishes and where necessary guards and maintains the local ecological heritage. Both kinds of personal leadership, internal and external co-operation, use and support of the County umbrella body, are employed in playing its public part. In addition it is an effective link in a larger network which includes cognate organisations and appropriate public services.

3. THROUGH PERVASIVE CHANGES AFFECTING THE QUALITY OF LIFE IN THE AREA AND
4. AFFECTING POLITICAL CONSCIOUSNESS, ACTIVITY AND STRUCTURE IN THE AREA

Ingleton CA, from a few scattered activities and inadequate facilities in a village divided into warring halves, and suffering from unemployment, weak adult education and youth work, has evolved a substantial and integrated community, arts, adult education, youth, sports and leisure complex, a united community, a vigorous tourist trade, a small industrial estate with jobs for the young, and various civic and political effects. Expert independent witnesses speak of civil society in Ingleton as uniquely active and effective in their experience. Our own evidence shows both overt and enabling leadership and internal and external co-operation at work, which make the local organisational network particularly dense. The organisation is an effective umbrella and provides wide-ranging opportunities for responsibility and civic training. Externally it links with all relevant public services at officer and politician levels, is a prolific source of personnel for local political office and assists analogous developments elsewhere.

The Guildhouse (see under 1 above) figures again here as an urban companion to Ingleton. Before the loss of core funding it had developed on comparable lines, had become the town's forum for concerned and responsible thinking about local, national and international issues, and provided opportunity for people to study these issues and make up their own minds. It was also active in a number of other broad directions; it founded Rugby's civic, arts and theatre societies. With hindsight it becomes clear that this LVO was fortunate in having, for a long time, professional staff who could be both inspiring leaders *and* enablers, and made it their business to train up as many others as they could lay their hand on in the whole spectrum of responsibility and leadership. It is not surprising that even external witnesses still attribute to the centre a degree of influence it seems to wield no longer.

The Arts Centre has to be considered jointly with the adult education centre which founded and continues to partner it. In addition to facilities for the practice and enjoyment of the arts, it provides the town with important facilities in which local people generally take much pride. These include the local tourist information office, a public meeting place with a refreshment service and a bar, gallery, exhibition spaces and meeting rooms. It is the centre for the enjoyment and teaching of the arts for a wide area, attracts professionals and sets standards for amateurs. There is modest professional staffing but every part of this large and complex organisation depends on voluntary service and is democratically governed. As a result the arts centre and its partner organisation provide an unusually large number of people with training in democratic responsibility as well as organisation and management. A notable proportion of people in public office has received its initiation into public service here, and (as at Ingleton) public participation in the democratic process is known to be above national and regional averages and particularly well informed. The centre is thus a major contributor to the high quality of local life and opportunities, and to a well developed civil society. All the available agencies – individual, co-operative, umbrella and network – are deployed in attaining this end.

The WI Group provides a varied range of facilities for its members. Additionally, it contributes substantially to every aspect of the quality of local life and to its political health through co-operation and networking with all other LVOs and the LA services. The training it provides in organising, management and civic responsibility means that, according to independent witnesses, two-thirds of the individuals who hold senior responsibility in local organisations and the civil parish are members of the WI. All forms of individual leadership, co-operation and networking are deployed but there is no evidence of any umbrella action.

Bassetlaw CVS with its various arms, especially the Self-Help Network, is source and focal point, organiser, initiator, trainer and encourager of LVOs in its area as well as an LVO in its own right. It makes direct provision for a variety of disadvantaged groups. Too complex to describe here (a reading of the case study and the Retford study is required for this) its impact on the quality of life in the area, on responsible civic activity and on well-informed political decision-making is influential. Through its teaching and information roles it gives overt leadership, but its enabling role in the founding, maintenance and energising of other LVOs is even more substantial. Co-operation and networking are the very essence of its activity.

The Settlement is, like Bassetlaw CVS and some others, an umbrella for a whole brood of LVOs under its wing. It provides formal education for those most in need and unable to profit from public provision. It prepares unemployed people for entry or re-entry into the labour market, and gives adults with learning difficulties their first chance ever. For all its members and sub-groups it is above all a safe haven in an exceedingly insecure and often dangerous environment. It also prepares them to understand and take a grip upon it by training potential local leaders (including some local councillors) in democratic citizenship and organising and management skills. It is thus a focus for values and quality in a seriously deprived community. For other organisations in the area it acts as a source of information and expertise, trainer and advocate. For local government officials it is an important source of information and a partner in public service. All individual, co-operative and networking skills are fully deployed.

Mountain Rescue sets an example of responsibility and public service which has no very great effect upon people resident in the immediate locality except in so far as a disproportionate number of Team members seem to be engaged in other forms of public service as well, to which they must have been elected by local people. However, the Team does have a great effect on the quality of facilities available to the visiting public through the environmental and mountaineering education and advice it furnishes to them and through the rescue work itself. Their leadership skills of both kinds are deployed in local civic activity as well as rescue and they co-operate closely within the organisation and externally with their partners in the public services, thus forming a dense and effective network.

The Residents' Association provides local people in general and its active members in particular with a general training in local civic understanding and action, in co-operation with each other, with other such associations under an area umbrella body, and in working with the LA. It has stimulated improvements to the physical environment, soothed some local tensions and spread habits of good neighbourliness. Leadership seems to be mainly overt and is much influenced by local councillors and officials, who also provide all the necessary organisational support. While it is effective in improving both the quality of life and the political skills and consciousness of local people, it is uncertain how far this LVO may have freed them to question their political and administrative masters' actions if they were to wish to do so.

Analysis of the Evidence

It is now practicable to tabulate this analysis in the same order, and using the alpha-numerical classification of agencies (cf. p. 121f. above). The Guildhouse receives a second entry which is based on reliable external evidence of its past condition. Information about those organisational characteristics which seemed to be notable or significant is added in the columns to the right.

It needs to be borne in mind that entries after each organisation's name define the paths which influence takes. Thus "Ujima 1 ab, 3" indicate *only the agency of contact or influence, and not the quality or quantity of these*. Thus (and without repeating the detailed analysis) in this example, the entry (whatever it may be and whether positive or negative) means that this organisation's impact is conveyed through the personalities of its own leaders, through organisational links, and via an umbrella body. The actual number of alpha-numerical entries after an organisation's name indicates the density of its network of communication. Finally, readers are asked to recall the caveat that the categorisations represent a snapshot at the time when each case study was executed. The characteristics of organisations will have differed both before and since it was taken.

The last two columns require elucidation. Under Relative Size organisations are described as large (L) in accordance with the glossary definition. However, a medium-sized or small group may be described as relatively large (rel.L) where it is large in proportion to its population catchment. Where size is immaterial the column is left blank. In the Staff column all entries are relative. Where no paid staff is employed the column is left blank.

This table delivers a number of interesting visual stimuli. Generally speaking the length of the string of letters and numbers after the title of each organisation increases from top to bottom and the x-marks form something very close to blocks in relation to the grouping. There are three exceptions. One (the Singers) is a small specialist organisation whose specialism has developed to such a degree that, though locally based, its stature and therefore the complexity and range of its influence, are well above this limited level. The second (Fifty-Plus) is very large, and the only generalist organisation in this block. The third (the Railway Trust), again, is very large, and its specialism, although clearly defined, is so multi-faceted and broadly influential that it could almost be regarded as a generalist organisation.

It was interesting to find that staffing or its absence appears to be of no importance in the context of impact on the local community. Size, on the other hand appeared to play a part and this will be brought into the overall discussion which follows analysis of the evidence. The number of members is not recorded in the table because what signifies is less a matter of absolute number than membership in proportion to catchment population. If this is taken into account then it will be seen that both the "transitional" pair and all those in the two most influential sub-groups (3 and 4 combined) are large. The sole exception (the Residents' Association) has few active members, but represents a large number. A further common factor is that most of these highly influential LVOs are generalist. Of the two exceptions, the Wildlife Trust's specialism includes public functions such as defence of important public interests and advocacy, while that of Mountain Rescue is multi-faceted. Of the three exceptions

Diagram 18: Case study organisations: effects on community, and agencies of this

A. Negative & Neutral Effects		SPEC	GEN	OUT	IN	DYN	STAT	DIV	REL SIZE	STAFF
Ujima	1ab,3		X	X				X		rel L
UIMWO	1ab,3,4		X	X				X	L	v L
W London CA	1ab		X	X				X	L	M
Rotary	1ab,3		X	X			X			
S Wales WEA	1ab,3		X		X		X			
B. Positive Effects										
1. Minor, individual										
NWR Group	1ab,2a		X		X	X				
Guildhouse	2a		X		X		X		L	rel S
Writers	2a,3,4	X			X		X			
Gardeners	2a	X			X		X		L	
Pigeon fanciers	2a	X			X		X			
PTA	1a	X			X		X			
2. Specific facilities, etc.										
Widows SH	1ab,2a	X			X		X			
Macular SH	1ab,3	X			X	X				
Patients' Cl.	1b,3	X		X		X				
Arthritis SH	1ab,3	X			X	X				
Archeologists	1ab,4	X			X		X			
Singers	1ab,2ab,4	X			X	X				v S
Fifty-Plus	1a,2a,3,4		X		X	X			L	
Railway Trust	1ab,2ab,4	X			X	X			L	L
Playgroup	1b,3	X			X	X				
Vol. Drivers	1b,3	X		X			X			
Aekta SH	1a,3	X			X	X				
2/3. Transition										
Kelvedon WEA	1ab,2ab,3,4		X		X		X		rel L	
Wildlife	1ab,2ab,3,4	X			X		X		L	
3. Pervasive, quality of life, inc. 2, &										
4. Affecting political consciousness, activity and structure										
Ingleton CA	1ab,2ab,3,4		X	X		X			L	v S
(Guildhouse, past)	(1ab,2ab,4)		(X)	(X)		(X)			L	S
Arts Centre	1ab,2ab,3,4		X	X		X			L	S
WI Group	1ab,2ab,3,4		X		X	X			rel L	
Bassetlaw CVS	1ab,2ab,3,4		X	X		X			L	M
Settlement	1ab,2ab,3,4		X	X		X			L	M
Mountain Rescue	1ab,2ab,3,4	X		X		X			rel L	
Residents	1ab,2ab,3,4		X		X		X			

in sub-group 2 the Singers and the Railway Trust are specialists, but the Singers have a strong value orientation and engage in public service, while the generalist aspects of the railwaymen's specialism have been noted.

The proportions of inward- to outward-looking orientation are also noteworthy. Of the 10 entries in the transitional and the most influential LVOs, six (all of them in sub-groups 3/4) have clearly outward objectives and four inward ones. The picture changes when these four are considered further. Kelvedon WEA, Wildlife Trust, WI Group and Residents are all classed as inward-looking because they exist to serve the particular interests of their members. All four of them, however, cause their members individually or as a group to undertake substantial and pervasive services to the community and, frequently, to take active or indeed leading parts in political life.

Finally, it will be noted that of the 13 most notably influential LVOs, 10 are in a dynamic stance and the other three, although in the static category, are very active indeed. All but one of them are also, as was shown in the previous chapter, among those whose members respond by a high level of participation and commitment to the great demands made on them by the organisation. Over one-third of the 51 respondents who were identified as leaders and innovators came from organisations in sub-groups 3 and 4. When the three exceptions from sub-group 2 (Singers, Fifty-Plus, Railway Trust) are added they have over half the leaders. This seems to point to the reciprocal impact of individuals and organisations.

Turning to the Negative and Neutral group it is noticeable that all five are generalist and either weakly static or divergent. Four are outward-looking and the one which looks inward has outward-looking pretensions. All have democratic constitutions but in only one of them (Rotary) is there any sense of widespread and active member participation, while one (the W London CA) has become effectively an autocracy.

Between these two extreme groups there are the two whose member LVOs influence the local community rather more modestly but regularly, either in limited ways or through the often imperceptible by-paths of individual transmission (Group B.1) and those which, in addition, provide the community with specific facilities and opportunities (B.2). As has been noted, three of this second sub-group do this on such a scale that their influence puts them on a level with those in the combined sub-group 3/4. Here again there are striking commonalities. All but three of the 17 LVOs in sub-groups B.1 and 2 are specialist, and all but two are inward-looking. All but one in sub-group B.1 are static and eight of the 11 in sub-group 2 are dynamic.

- In summary, the case study evidence suggests that the most striking influence on communities comes from LVOs which are dynamic, generalist, and well-endowed with leaders and innovators. However, dynamic specialist LVOs, well-led, can also exert substantial and enduring influence. In general specialist LVOs which are static and in good heart tend to make their impact in a less direct fashion and often through the provision of facilities.

Retford Evidence

The evidence which has been presented so far shows that those organisations which made the most impact on the community at large were also most closely linked, through co-operation and networking, with other LVOs. The whole subject of inter-organisational relationships is the raison d'être of the Retford locality study (Reynolds, *et al.*, 1994), and readers are referred to this for a detailed and individually illustrated account of these interactive processes.

Networking depends on links, and its effectiveness on the use to which these are put. Information is useful, especially where it travels both ways. More important are ideas, energy, resources and mutual services. Most of this requires personal interaction, and the Retford evidence shows how multiple memberships and other activities of individuals contribute to the network which links organisations. Generally speaking, the evidence shows that the denser the network, the greater the impact which every organisation within it makes, and receives.

Interaction, whether between LVOs only or between them and the public or other sectors, is quantifiable as was shown in the Retford study. However, interaction is not, by itself, a positive influence on the life of a community, nor can the quality of life or contributions to it be measured although they can be described and assessed impressionistically. On the other hand interaction is necessary for a positive influence to be conveyed, and its quality and quantity are therefore significant. The Retford evidence shows it to be generally very strong and there are important differences according to organisational objectives, with some interesting exceptions. These last are found among two kinds of inward-looking groups. One consists of purely sociable LVOs which tend to be insular because self-sufficient. The other includes small specialist LVOs which are self-sufficient because either they possess whatever facilities they require or, more often, they do not need any. It should not be supposed that because they are insular such organisations do not contribute to the community's quality of life: for example, a few, usually large, social organisations for old people and the many, usually small, darts teams clearly do, but their influence is relatively narrowly channelled.

By contrast, the main body of evidence shows substantial interaction, with significant differences. Approximately equal numbers of inward- and outward-looking organisations had *some* links with the statutory sector. However, these links were weak for about a quarter of the inward-looking organisations and strong for four-fifths of the outward-looking ones. The complex interaction of the effects of organisational objectives, staffing and funding is explained in Reynolds *et al.* (1994, p. 32f.) Its main conclusion for the present purpose is that the link between objectives, size and funding is fundamental here rather than that between staffing and relationships. The reason is that it is large and outward-looking organisations which tend to require staff, and staff salaries are the main consumers of funding. However, once staff are employed both the need for negotiations and the availability of personnel stimulate the growth of relationships in all directions.

Outward-looking groups (of which the majority are generalist) are thus in a stronger position to make an *overt* impact upon public issues and the visible quality of life in an area, than inward-looking ones. Inward-looking LVOs are no less effective, but more often they make their impact implicitly, indirectly and on a narrower front determined by their main organisational objectives and any facilities they happen to command. Moreover, our earlier analysis of the case study evidence shows that those inward-looking or specialist groups (e.g. WI Group, Wildlife Trust, Widows SH) whose activities involve issues of public or political interest and which are strongly participative, make as strong an overt impact as the most influential of the outward-looking generalists.

Retford is, in some respects, a special case because of the way in which this positive interplay among LVOs and between them and the statutory and other sectors is deliberately and energetically fostered by the Bassetlaw District Council's (BDC) policy. This recognises both the independence and the complementary role of VOs and seeks to support them in both with encouragement, facilities and resources. In particular the importance of core funding as a safeguard for forward planning and co-operation is recognised. Together with the County Council the BDC funds the local CVS with its Self-Help Link. The details of the policy and its consequences for the development of voluntary activity and social development are described in detail in Reynolds *et al.* (1994, pp. 10–14). This also makes the point that the policy owes much to the considerable number of local Councillors who received their early training in active citizenship in local VOs before being elected to public office. The same link between earlier training in VOs and subsequent service in the public sphere emerged in eight of the case studies (Ingleton CA, Guildhouse, the Arts Centre, the WI Group, the Railway Trust, the Settlement, Mountain Rescue and the Wildlife Trust).

The key to all this and much more is that BDC's objective is "as much to enable and empower people to do things themselves and be responsible for them as to make direct provision, ... (and) to create unlimited and powerful opportunities for citizens to have clearer and more direct access to the decision-making process."

The importance of the local CVS to the practice of co-operation between the LA and the voluntary sector and to the nurture of active citizenship, emerges clearly. Together with its Self-Help Link Bassetlaw CVS is intended to be the focal point for the whole network, source of expertise and advice for the statutory authorities no less than the LVOs, and as an arm's length tool for public funding and practical assistance to be channelled to organisations whose autonomy is important. Reynolds *et al.* (1994) and the case study in Stewart *et al.* (1992) present detailed evidence on how all this is achieved, and its outcomes.

There is no other instance where we have been aware of such systematic policies aimed at maximising the positive influence of the voluntary sector on public affairs and the quality of life. However, strong parallels among the individual case study organisations are notable, and co-operation between all the sectors is particularly intimate and effective in the case of Ingleton. What distinguishes all these and Retford is the recognition that LVOs have the potential for making unique contributions of their own. The public sector can welcome and foster that contribution, and no doubt does so in some places we do not happen to have studied. If it tries to take it over for its own purposes it destroys the potential and, very likely, harms the quality of what is offered. Reynolds *et al.* (1994) is again relevant:

> *the declared policy of the BDC and of BCVS, Action Centre and Self-Help Link is to assist people in groups (wherever appropriate) to identify their own need, intentions and potential, and to provide them with whatever support, advice, facilities or resources they may need to meet them by their own autonomous efforts. All our evidence suggests that this policy of community development or (in current jargon) empowerment is also their practice. The effect is a burgeoning voluntary sector alive with thoughtful, active and responsible citizens, which acts independently and co-operates successfully with Local Government. So far, at least, there appear to have been no attempts to shed public responsibility and compromise voluntary effort by sucking it into a contract culture. This is a fortunate contrast to the widespread damage reported by Knight (1993) and in our earlier findings, both published (Case Study 17) and unpublished. Up to the present the voluntary sector in Retford, and presumably Bassetlaw, has been spared the misfortune of being starved into surrendering its birthright and its civic duty for a mess of contracts (p. 41).*

Conclusion

- The great majority of LVOs make a positive impact on the character and the quality of life of their local communities, and some of the most effective are more than locally influential.

- This influence may vary in kind and in the routes it takes as well as in content and effect. The ripples caused by a seemingly unknown and apparently private LVO's effect (e.g. the NWR Group) may turn up anonymously and by circuitous routes in the public domain.

- High levels of interaction and networking, supported by a positive but arms-length LA policy fostering a mutuality of voluntary and statutory effort, relate closely to effectiveness of impact on quality of life and an active civil society.

- LVOs employing paid staff are likely to have stronger links with the statutory sector, but the force and quality of an LVO's impact beyond itself does not depend on possession of paid staff. It *is* affected by the quality of leadership, paid or unpaid. Where leadership is enabling and co-operative, organisations develop more effectively for the public good than where it is authoritarian and isolationist.

- LVOs with an enabling leadership and a participative democratic structure, which are generalist and have a variety of interests and activities, and whose activities involve the practice of discussion and the consideration of values and standards, contribute the largest number of trained personnel to the democratic and organisational requirements of the public sphere. They make an identifiable contribution to active citizenship and civil society in their area, and offer a model to others.

We have now summarised our findings about the nature and influence of learning and development in individuals and in groups, and the impact of LVOs on their surrounding communities. Our evidence on some of the important processes which may foster, or hinder, such learning and development, is considered in the next chapter.

Chapter 9

Processes and Outcomes

The preceding chapters have considered individual learning, individuals and groups, organisational learning and development, and the effect of all these upon communities. This chapter considers the project's findings on how some processes, relationships and organisational structures facilitated or, occasionally, hindered the ability of LVOs to function optimally and exert whatever beneficial influence may have been appropriate to their objectives and practicable in their circumstances. It has been necessary to touch upon these subjects in preceding chapters. Some have probably been dealt with adequately in these other contexts and need only be mentioned briefly now; others still await the presentation and discussion of evidence. This will be ordered in a sequence which moves from the personal end of the spectrum to organisational issues, the nature of leadership, staffing, lay–professional relationships, and matters of structure and constitution.

The Effect of Personal Relationships Within the Group

This topic has emerged so frequently in preceding discussion that only a summary is needed here. Warm relationships, mutual support and caring were found, throughout all the investigations and with every kind of activity and respondent, to have been the source of LVOs' success in building up the confidence of individual members. For almost everyone they were the foundation upon which all subsequent learning and development was built. In particular the quality of such relationships was found to be a crucial factor in enabling those individuals who would not otherwise have been expected to do so, to overcome educational and social barriers to learning. Competing ambitions which led to conflict among leading members were an important cause of the collapse of an organisation, which the project happened to witness.

Activity, Demands, Continuity and Commitment

Throughout the project's fieldwork a clear relationship emerged between the kind and level of demands which an organisation made upon its members, the energy of their response, and the success of the organisation. Organisations which involved or required active rather than passive forms of participation had a stronger hold upon their memberships, and their members reported more learning and personal change. Within organisations those members who took on the most active or demanding tasks also showed the most distinctive learning curves. This was equally noticeable in some practical activities, like the Railway Trust, and in more abstract ones such as the Kelvedon WEA.

The more energetically members were contributing to and consequently learning in their LVO's activity, the greater their commitment; the greater that commitment the more they were found to learn and to develop. Moreover, there seemed to be no obvious distinction between commitment to the organisation and its activities and mutual commitment to fellow members. In groups which appeared to exemplify this tendency to a high degree, such as the Singers or the WI Group, there was no way in which a distinction between commitment to organisational objectives, activity and inter-personal relationships could have been drawn.

Continuity or frequent succession of challenges was found to play an important part in maintaining the dynamism or constructive stasis of organisations and the learning behaviour of their members. This could take many different forms, depending on the characteristics of the organisation. In a small self-help group like Widows SH, once it was established, new challenges would continually arrive in the shape of new members needing help, or new legislation affecting them. In large and complex organisations such as the Railway Trust or Bassetlaw CVS expansion into new projects and services kept up the creative tension, while new content as among the Writers and the continuous striving for higher standards by the Singers achieved the same effects.

Conversely, those organisations which demanded little from their members, regardless of what they might have offered to them, seemed also to make less impact upon them. Little evidence of learning and personal change was found among members of such LVOs, and the organisations themselves were found to exhibit characteristics which placed them at the negative end of the static or squarely in the divergent category.

Democratic Responsibility

All but one of the case study organisations and the great majority of those Retford LVOs which were identified had democratic constitutions or frameworks. In practice the exceptional case study turned out to be extremely informal, with widely dispersed responsibility. On the other hand three case study LVOs with theoretically democratic constitutions and some of the Retford organisations of the voluntary agency type had ceased to be democratic, or had never been in that category. Having a democratic constitution did not mean that an LVO was necessarily a very active democracy. However, respondents were at least aware of "owning" their LVO, of its autonomy, and of the fact that it was their votes which placed committee members and others in positions of responsibility. Members share the power to change policy and sometimes use it.

More often than not consciousness of democratic values went deeper and participation was high. Especially in small organisations a high proportion of members held some kind of responsibility. The high proportion of respondents who discharge elected office and other responsible duties has been reported earlier (cf. p. 70ff. above). Responsibility within an organisation is, of course, simply a specialised form of commitment to it and to the service of fellow members. As such it could be expected to have similar consequences for personal learning and development, and this proved to be the case. Those who bore such responsibility also commonly showed themselves to be more committed, to have learned and developed more strongly in all the categories under which the evidence was presented in Chapter 5.

The effects of commitment were thus not only personal and internal to the organisation concerned. Those who took on responsibilities and had learned more in other respects were also more aware of broader social concerns, to have engaged in what we call political learning, and to undertake consequential action.

- There is thus a direct relationship between the mode of government of an LVO and its contribution to local leadership and the level of active citizenship in an area.

Since the vast majority of LVOs are democratic and many of them effectively so, the project was able to demonstrate this relationship in at least half of its fieldwork and provide important independent evidence in a several instances.

Leaders and Leadership

Individuals from among the respondents in each case study organisation who emerged clearly as having a leadership or innovatory role were listed. Office holders who did not, in practice, discharge such a role were excluded. The list includes a variety of styles – commanding figures as well as enablers, facilitators and innovators, delegators and autocrats. Moreover, people had not always been leaders, but had grown (or been thrust) into that role, in some instances, from unexpected beginnings and backgrounds. Neither did they adopt just one particular style of leadership. Many of them had developed from one to another and a few had learned to adopt different styles from a repertoire to suit the need of the moment.

A surprising feature of the attempt to identify the characteristics of the group of leaders and innovators was that they did not, in essence, differ very much from those of respondents in general. One-third (rather more than the proportion for the whole sample) had been educated beyond the age of 19. Few seemed to exhibit outstanding talent and vitality, or to lack them to a comparable degree. Certain organisations spread the leadership role very widely indeed among their members, either from necessity (like the Railway Trust, Mountain Rescue or any mature self-help group) or as a matter of policy (all the women's organisations, the Singers).

When the effects of turnover are added to this it begins to look as if there was no such thing as a "born leader": given a supportive, learning and *un*competitive organisational environment in which experience can be gathered, it seems that a very high proportion of members will naturally blossom into responsible and leadership roles of one kind or another. Our evidence suggests, indeed, that it is absence of competition which enables people to rise and use their talents who have not been aware of their own potential, and who would refuse to fight their way up. This is not to suggest that exceptional talents and energies do not exist. Where they do they are unmistakeable, but they are not common enough to occur in more than a minority of organisations at any one time. What our findings do suggest is that the *potential* leadership pool in any group is far wider and deeper than is often imagined, and that co-operation and nurturing are more likely than competition to bring hidden talent into the light of day. We shall return to this subject when we come to discuss common problems in securing succession. Meanwhile it is tempting to note that the same factors operate here as were found to be important in what was proposed as the "Sibsey effect" on pp. 62–65 above.

It is interesting to trace the apparent effects of the variety of leadership styles and roles identified during fieldwork within the range of environments in which they were observed. There was just one instance of autocracy (W London CA). Its effect was to reverse the group's learning and development and reduce its usefulness. It is, however, impossible to generalise from this, since there is no means of knowing what would have been the result in that particular environment if autocratic management had been exercised to different ends and with other talents. Given the UIMWO's policy decision to concentrate on contract finance, a business managerial leadership style, including delegation to similar under-managers, must have been logical. However, it made a hierarchical structure inevitable, and analogous styles and attitudes natural all the way down the ladder. The sea-change from members to clients, from learning and responsibility to deference, was an obvious consequence.

The Guildhouse, as another large organisation, provided an interesting contrast. When forced to dispense with professional leadership, the members decided to carry on by dividing the warden's functions among the elected committee members. Each was to gather round her- or himself a sub-committee of helpers. Each found that to launch and maintain their new role they had to engage in rapid learning, and create an active momentum for their committee. This they did by taking on the whole task themselves initially and then handing over such parts of it as they could to members of their committee.

The outcome is wide dispersal of responsibility for policy-making and execution, with its concomitant developmental effect on the leading individuals and their sub-committee members. It intensifies the quality of commitment to the organisation of a large number of people, and enhances their learning processes. However, the outcome also suggests some interesting aspects of the relationship between members and staff, professional and lay roles, which will be discussed shortly.

Wide dispersal, commitment and practical example are thus cardinal aspects of the leadership style adopted at the Guildhouse. The same characteristics, combined with enabling skills and sensitive personal support, characterise leadership in some of the self help groups, the Bassetlaw Self-Help Network, and the NWR Group. Of the other women's groups the Widows' leadership adds the more overt authority of an advocate and public representative, while the internal and external complexities of WI and village structures demand the organisational flair for which that organisation is famous.

Where a democratic and self-governing organisation employs professional staff the problems of leadership become yet more complex. They may be multiplied where a professional's loyalties are divided between the organisation and some outside body, or (in rare instances) at variance with what might be regarded as good practice. Other negative aspects were discussed on pp. 18f. above.

Staff and Volunteers, Professionals and Lay Officers

A very different range of problems *can* arise in the different circumstances of voluntary agencies and volunteer employing agencies, where paid staff, usually professionals or para-professionals, are appointed from outside the group, to be in charge of local volunteers recruited to do the agency's work. Organisations of this kind were excluded from the case study sample by our working definition of an LVO, but included in the Retford remit. Some of the responses there indicate the risks to which such structures are exposed, and possible reasons why some of these agencies find recruitment difficult.

Among LVOs proper the project sample includes 13 LVOs which employ staff. Among these six very different organisations had found successful solutions to the problem of relationship between paid staff and volunteers, and professional and lay (or amateur) service. An attempt to describe relevant aspects of each of these and analyse them should reveal useful generalisations about the relationship, and some perceptions on the role and styles of leadership in voluntary groups.

The Railway Trust runs technical services which are potentially dangerous and subject to stringent, legally enforced, standards. The services are linked to heritage activities, complex equipment, ownership of extensive property and a substantial commercial operation. They must be managed by individuals who possess recognised and legally valid expertise in all these fields. A growing number of such tasks have become too large for volunteer rotas and require the undivided attention of full-time and qualified personnel. Since the necessary expertise exists among the leading volunteers these have been appointed to such posts, and new paid appointments, both full- and part-time, are being made from the same source.

However, some senior personnel thus appointed also retain elected office and serve in that capacity. Coming from appropriate backgrounds of experience, they found themselves adopting the hierarchical relationships to which they were used, with other officers and committee members and with the volunteers. However, the organisation also has a complex and effective system of democratically elected committees and sub-committees in which numerous members are being trained up in democratic responsibility. Working within this structure, executives soon realised that in their new voluntary context professional standards of work have to be combined with an enabling style of leadership. Nevertheless there is some evidence of occasional discontent due to the fact that some individuals are being paid for work (albeit on a full-time basis) which the majority are doing voluntarily in their leisure time. Such jealousies may be an insoluble precipitate of human frailty, but it may be helpful to introduce a constitutional distinction between paid executives and elected members into the upper echelon of the structure.

In the smaller and much less complex context of the Playgroup the problem identified in good time at the Railway Trust had, at one time in its history, become serious. There the original playgroup supervisor had assumed full authority over the group's policy and management, to the extent of excluding committee members and other parents. Her eventual replacement adopts a more appropriate style, recognising the distinction between the paid professional's advisory and executive role and the committee's policy-making and managerial one. Volunteering has been revived, a parent rota assists in running the group and, implicitly, provides the parent education which exclusion had frustrated.

The Arts Centre provides teaching in the practice and appreciation of the arts and crafts both in its own right and jointly with its founder and partner, the adult education centre. It also provides performances and exhibitions at professional level, and it acts as an umbrella organisation for other voluntary organisations most of which are devoted to the amateur practice of the arts. The membership and the very large force of volunteers are drawn from all these sources, and the governing committees and sub-committees represent all of them. They include highly experienced individuals who have given many years of service and may be in charge of important aspects of the work as well as the resources which these require and consume.

Owing to an unusually low level of public funding the centre is forced to appoint professional staff on the basis of promise rather than the proven experience appropriate to senior posts in an organisation of this size and importance. The task is to provide professional advice, standards, organisation and teaching among the complexities of the organisation which has been described. It is usually undertaken by very young people, mostly without much experience or background as yet, and not uncommonly after an interregnum during which volunteers have done their best to fill the gap.

There is unusual potential here for conflict or disappointment. There is also a tradition, rooted in the centre's adult education origins, of egalitarianism, mutual supportiveness, and the sense of a collective for learning. It was fascinating, during the case study, to observe the careful respect with which established voluntary officers with experience of filling professional gaps supported the authority of recently appointed professional staff, and the tact with which they guided them into the skilled execution of their responsibilities. The response was quick and confident learning and the assumption of dedicated professional values and standards of work.

Two areas of skill seemed to take longer to acquire. One is the kind of educative diplomacy needed to find ways of bringing these standards to bear upon the work of affiliated amateur groups. The other is appreciation of the educational and political importance of nurturing and exploiting the strength of the small army of members and volunteers on whom the special quality of the structure rests. Professional staff coming new to voluntary organisations cannot fail to recognise the visible importance of experienced voluntary officers and managers of particular activities in evolving policy and providing continuity. What may be easy to miss is the responsibility for developing, encouraging and continually recruiting the membership at large which throws up the common-and-garden volunteers as well as the leadership. This centre thus requires a whole repertoire of leadership styles both from its voluntary officers and from its professional staff, as well as the sensitivity that enables them to vary their methods as experience is being gained and relationships change.

The Bassetlaw CVS presents comparable but subtly different problems and solutions. Like the Arts Centre it is both a direct provider and an umbrella for other organisations which are affiliated but independent. However, it also has important advisory and representative roles. Innovation, especially by means of continual enquiry into needs and the stimulation of new activities, organisations and services, is important among these. As an honest broker between public authorities and the voluntary sector, it has diplomatic and political functions, and it dispenses financial aid. Here the relationship between paid professional staff and the senior and experienced volunteers likely to be found in committees is closer to that between senior professional officers in local government and elected members. Duties and boundaries are well defined and mostly understood by all concerned.

On the other hand the direct provision of such a complex organisation calls for the variety of leadership roles it demonstrates. Its adult education provision demands the tutorial leadership of a centre warden. The social service and innovation role deploys research and survey skills but also those of the enabler and facilitator who, on discovering the rich potential of another's plot of land, quietly fertilises and sows it, and returns later to congratulate the owner on the crop.

The two remaining organisations furnish different ways of illuminating the topic. In the case of the Singers the role of the conductor as the single professional working with amateur members was outlined on p. 112f. above. A fascinating and mostly verbatim account appears in the original case study in Stewart *et al.* (1992), pp. 184–201. Here the stress is both on total social integration and careful distinction between organisational and professional leadership. However, the conductor regards himself as a member on a par with the rest, and recognises that ultimately his professional policy decisions must be subject to discussion and criticism. But these potential sources of conflict are safely ignored because both conductor and members are aware of the mutual challenge towards higher standards and wider repertoire which unites them in a learning spiral within which learning and cultural experience, social interaction and demanding commitment, react upon each other. The original case study sees this as "an effective instance of resolving (and) turning to constructive account the role tensions in the relationship between a professional and the members of a VO. It depends ... on fostering among the membership an attitude of confidence and independence which rests on a foundation of competence and good relationships (and) the professional himself ensures that professional policy is ... discussed with members, and subject to their ultimate democratic control."

The original note argues that, while easier to achieve in such a small organisation, smallness is no guarantee of success, and it refers to evidence from the Arts Centre and certain other adult education and community centres to show that, given necessarily more elaborate structures, "the same constructive relationships between professionals and membership can be achieved in larger organisations".

The Settlement differs from all the others in this group in so far as events, to which the organisation could do no more than react as constructively as possible, forced it into something very near a dissolution rather than a bridging of the divide between staff and volunteer, professional and lay roles (cf. p. 69f. above). The Case Study related the Settlement's experience to comparable findings from, especially, Ingleton CA, the Guildhouse, the Arts Centre, the Singers and the Railway Trust and suggested that a synthesis led to an understanding of "what makes for constructive relationships between staff and volunteer, professionals and lay people, paid and unpaid, leader and member, client and user" in VOs. It identified three characteristics which seemed to underlie such relationships:

- an absence of any feeling of hierarchy, a genuine egalitarianism which was unaffected by the obvious differences in levels of responsibility borne by different individuals
- the absence of distinctions or symbols of status attached to either the type of employment ... or the actual task undertaken
- the pervasive sense that "leadership" was exerted modestly by example ... rather than aggressively by demands.

The egalitarianism which (at the Settlement) has senior staff, members of council and members or volunteers sharing the washing-up may be less easy to achieve in organisations which are not quite so poor, but the principle, and those of warm support within the group, of sharing, respect and example seem to be universal.

The examples reported in various LVOs, of remarkable leadership by individuals who seemed not to be greatly exceptional, and hardly prepared for it, are notable. They confirm earlier findings (cf. p. 139f. above) that a much greater proportion of people than is commonly assumed may be capable of demanding commitments, responsibility, and leadership. VOs, because of their supportive attitudes and habit of co-operation, make it more likely that the potential will be discovered and fostered. There is no denying that other styles of leadership exist, and may be needed in special circumstances even by LVOs: a world without heroes would be a poorer place. Example is always needed, but our evidence, and other experience, suggest that, by and large, LVOs and their members respond more positively to nurturing and enabling styles than to dominant authority.

Some organisations experienced difficulty in securing succession to responsibilities such as office or committee membership. These were invariably LVOs which had been established for some time, which had been well served by their leaders for much of that period, and which had no rule limiting the tenure of office. They were anxious to secure change, but seemed to know of no way of achieving it other than to ask for volunteers at general meetings. People rarely put themselves forward in such circumstances.

Limits on tenure help by forcing the issue, but the most successful organisations are those which make sensitive arrangements to approach individuals, ask them to help existing office holders and find out more about the task, prior to allowing themselves to be nominated with the prospect of being well prepared for their new responsibilities, and welcomed to them. Co-operation and nurture rather than sudden demands were found to be most successful in discovering leaders and ensuring succession in all positions of responsibility. Organisations like the Railway Trust, the WI Group, the Arts Centre or the Settlement and Mountain Rescue, which disperse responsibility widely and ensure that everyone who can be persuaded has experience of it, are naturally more successful in this than others. They seem to have no difficulty in securing turnover and developing the talents of their members.

The apparent experience that this happens fairly commonly in organisations whose objectives are internal to themselves, such as those we define as LVOs, but more rarely in the agency type of organisation now explains itself. Where objectives, ultimate responsibility and control are external and imposed, people can, at best, serve a cause, but they cannot own it.

There are no panaceas in the world of LVOs any more than anywhere else. Models of success can and must vary according to circumstances and personalities. They depend upon the objectives being pursued, on the content of the activity, and on the set of values deliberately (as in the case of Pigeon Fanciers or Singers) or implicitly (as by the Writers or Patients' Support) being applied to the standards of what is being undertaken. But there do seem to be some commonalities of a rather general order. Our evidence suggests that LVOs are most likely to succeed in their endeavours:

- As a result of a general practice of acceptance, support, fostering, nurturing and teaching, combined with maximum demands for active commitment.

- If there is respect for the personality and potential of every member, and maximum demands are made for their active participation.

- If they are democratic and practise the widest possible dispersal of responsibility among the membership and the development of their talents in co-operation, rather than competition.

- If leaders quietly set standards through personal example, and eschew the forms and symbols of status and hierarchy.

- If, where staff are employed, a clear and sensible understanding of staff and voluntary officers' respective roles and functions is established, and any boundaries are approached with sensitivity and mutual respect.

Chapter 10

Some Implications of the Findings

Introductory

The project's findings demonstrate that most LVOs have important and constructive functions. They make crucial contributions to the nation's morale, to its social, economic, political and cultural vitality, and thus to the overall quality of its life (Chapters 8, 9). Since it has been shown that the project's statistics are capable of extrapolation to national estimates, the overall scale of the LVOs' contribution can be indicated: there are about 1.3 million LVOs and their membership is likely to exceed 30 million individuals (Chapter 3).

LVOs make their contribution by means of the implicit and explicit learning and personal development of their individual members (Chapters 4, 5, 6) and the development of groups (Chapter 7), by the transmission of learning and change from individuals and groups to their contacts in home, neighbourhood, interest communities and work places throughout their catchment areas and sometimes beyond (Chapters 5, 7, 8). Because they are independent and self-governing and depend on their members' co-operation, they foster the skills and the responsibilities of independence, self-government and co-operation. They are thus both nurseries and channels for active citizenship in a democratic society, and an important training ground for public service and public office (Chapter 8).

Their contribution to the economy is threefold: at the simplest level they improve many of their members' occupational effectiveness in a variety of ways (Chapter 5). Secondly, abundant medical and social services evidence shows that their contribution to the maintenance or improvement of members' physical and mental health, and to their ability to cope with problems and crises, is so great as to save substantial public expenditure (Chapters 5, 8). Thirdly, they create many of the most fully used and appreciated opportunities and facilities needed for civilised and healthy ways of life. Their contribution to the quality of any community's life substantially raises its morale and therefore its vitality (Chapter 8).

Voluntary organisations are therefore strong *net* contributors to the public good, and to the overall wellbeing of the nation, to its good government and its economy. They offer to local government and local public services a source of information and ideas on the state, the needs, the morale and the ethos of the community, and on its needs. Nobody and nothing other than voluntary organisations can make these particular contributions to the public good, and communities are irretrievably impoverished by their diminution or loss.

Implications for Voluntary Organisations

In Relation to their Members

A voluntary organisation is, and belongs to, its members. It exists to meet their needs and objectives, pursue their interests, expand their potential. It does not belong to, or exist for the benefit of its officers, or any outside body, or the state, whether or not it happens to be a source of grant or help.

To succeed in its task, it needs to create a warm, personally caring and supportive network of relationships which respects the personality and needs of each member. Its arrangements have to encourage individual members to feel that they own, have ultimate responsibility for and are personally involved in the organisation. To secure this it must both respond to its members' needs and interests, and demonstrate its own need of their contribution. It stretches them through responsible and demandingly active participation, and by helping them to be aware of the organisation's needs, problems and opportunities (Chapters 4–7).

It is relatively easy to achieve these objectives during an organisation's early life. To maintain them, arrangements are needed to provide a continuity of worthwhile challenges and opportunities for progression in the chosen activity or interest, as well as the enjoyment of its benefits. Discussion and critical thinking have their place in all kinds of groups. All, regardless of their particular content, have the potential to be collectives for learning, and capable of delivering the three kinds of adult learning listed on p. 52 as personal, social and general education.

All voluntary organisations, therefore, are potentially, and ought to become, training grounds for active citizens.

Structures

In both structure and constitutional practice a voluntary organisation ought to be a pattern in miniature of what a working democracy should be like.

Organisations need to ensure that membership is understood to mean commitment, and that all representative office is genuinely elective. The more widely responsibility is dispersed within an organisation, the stronger the involvement and commitment of members and the more widespread the development of social and political learning among them. Dispersal of responsibility also facilitates a healthy turnover of office holders, and provides training and experience to ensure smooth and regular succession (Chapter 9).

Sound management, however it is structured, invariably improves an organisation's ability to serve its members. Once established, it saves time and tempers. Leadership, whether lay and voluntary or paid, or professional, is best conceived as a creative, enabling and nurturing role, not a dominant and authoritarian one. However competitive an organisation's activities may be, *internally* it thrives best on co-operation (Chapter 9).

The different roles of members, volunteers and elected officers, and

those of employed staff, need to be recognised, appreciated and reinforced through mutual support. Especially where professional staff is
employed, it is essential that constitutional structures (or at least recognised practice) should discriminate between its members' expert advisory and executive roles and the governing and policy-making ones of
elected officers and committee members (Chapters 2, 7–9).

External Relationships

A voluntary organisation is one expression among many of the ethos
and the vitality of its community. It does not stand on its own, and is
likely to share its individual members with other organisations, with local politics, the public services, business and industry and the professions. This means that it is, potentially, both easy and beneficial for it to
seek maximum contact and co-operation with all of these, remembering
that co-operation means literally working together and involves both
giving and receiving. Umbrella or intermediary bodies which we have
found playing such a constructive part, are the outcome of this policy of
sharing.

At the same time an organisation needs to maintain clear awareness
of its own objectives and of optimal ways of making its own proper contribution to the service of its members and, through them or directly
(whichever may be appropriate) to the community's quality of life. Responsibilities beyond its own concerns follow if it is in receipt of financial
aid or help in kind from public sources, especially if the organisation is
engaged in some form of public service. The benefits may be essential to
its work and its continued existence. However, a voluntary organisation
needs to wield a very long spoon when considering whether to sup the
mess of pottage offered by service contracts (Chapters 8, 9).

Implications for Local Policy and Action

LAs should recognise the role of VOs, the benefits they confer on people,
and their practical value to themselves and their own and other local
public services. This value will remain largely potential unless and until
the LA evolves a constructive and realistic policy towards the voluntary
sector and helps to ensure its realisation, supervision, evaluation and appropriate development. Such a policy must include financial and other
practical elements. VOs are more than convenient and economical for the
statutory sector. Our case studies demonstrate that they are *better* able to
carry out *some* functions than the public service, and they discharge some
functions which the public service *cannot* discharge. Conversely, LAs
need to recognise that there are some functions which VOs cannot discharge effectively, or at all. A policy on VOs will therefore be of little
value to the authority unless it also includes arrangements for *mutual*
consultation, for joint training, and sharing of advice and information
(Chapter 8).

The majority of LVOs (as opposed to voluntary agencies and the
like) need no financial help, but some need modest help in kind. This

may include free or subsidised accommodation (including facilities such as pitches and storage), or help with services such as duplicating and publicity. All LVOs benefit from, and are encouraged by, civic recognition and the public acknowledgment this confers upon them (Chapter 8).

Certain organisations, however, cannot deliver their service without relatively substantial funding which normally can only come from public sources. Occasionally this may mean a capital grant for a specific purpose. More commonly public funding is needed for the salaries and expenses of professional and other staff. Where such regular maintenance grants are needed, their most important and most beneficial form is core funding. It is, of course, highly desirable that this should be guaranteed for a reasonable period rather than subject to precarious annual reviews. Core funding enables both the LA and the VO to plan ahead. It also creates a reliable foundation on which the VO can earn or seek additional funds for additional work (Chapter 8).

Many functions such as investigation of social, cultural and financial needs in a community, or innovation, planning, stimulating new developments, assessing and delivering small-scale grant aid and services, training, networking and related publicity, are essential to an efficient and civilised community. They would be prohibitively expensive and very difficult for an LA to undertake by itself. Yet these functions can be carried out efficiently and economically if undertaken by a generalist intermediary body. This is normally a CVS, set up jointly by the LA and the voluntary sector as an LVO in its own right, to ensure constructive liaison between all concerned and undertake the functions which have been outlined. There ought to be one in every LA's area (Chapter 8).

All LAs and public services are today under pressure to contract out services. Because VOs are almost always poor and are becoming poorer due to the disappearance of core funding, they are tempted to compete for contracts; because they are able to call upon the services of volunteers they can often win them; because standards are less rigorously enforced than in the past they tend to spiral down a succession of short-term contracts. LAs may be forced into this contract culture, but they are well advised to consider most carefully and selectively whether to invite VOs to join them in it. The GONGO (Rajesh Tandon's "government-organised non-government organisation") is neither an efficient nor, in the long-run, an economical means of delivering services; it destroys the organisation's own potential to carry out its proper functions, strikes at the roots of its independence, and leaves the community impoverished under the pretence of having saved money.

LAs have little room for manoeuvre in trying to mitigate the dire effects of recent legislation upon voluntary adult education in all its forms. What little can be done by them – for instance by the restoration of affiliation schemes – can make disproportionately important contributions to the voluntary sector and to the survival, or strengthening, of active citizenship (Chapter 8).

Implications for National Policy and Action

Our study of *local* voluntary organisations, including autonomous local branches of big national organisations, and our findings about them, entitle us to speak of all these, but not of the large centralised agencies and charities.

Our findings have shown that *in certain specific areas* of service and activity voluntary organisations are superior to direct statutory provision. There are, indeed, many functions which only they can perform. To assume that local (and indeed central) government can manage without the voluntary sector is to look to the kind of societies which have collapsed in Eastern Europe. Conversely, to assume that functions which are rightly the responsibility of democratically accountable professional public services can be contracted out to the voluntary sector without any harm being suffered anywhere is a vulgar error.

On our evidence there would be advantage to any national government looking beyond the immediate future in considering these matters. National government has no less need of communication, information and informed advice than local government. In the context of our own remit, its task is to enable local government and local public services to be effective, well informed and economical, and to furnish them with the means to create in their bailiwick a high quality of life based on an active civil society. In so far as this involves LVOs this means that central government needs to be active in four areas:

1. It needs to ensure that LAs and centrally controlled local services have the funds to enable them to give appropriate and continuing support to LVOs on a reliable basis, allowing for adequate rolling plans. In particular it should require all LAs to sponsor the creation of councils of voluntary services and provide for this in settling their finances.
2. It should reverse policies which have the destructive effect of reducing the funding available to LAs for these purposes, and those policies which tend to divert LVOs from their proper tasks and into substitution for public services.
3. It should restore to LVOs, including voluntary adult education in all its forms, the means of equipping the adult population with the knowledge, understanding and skills required by a civilised nation, and an active civil society, by reversing policies which caused the collapse of the system of general adult education.
4. It should give careful consideration to and seek advice on provision to meet the staffing and training needs of VOs, and ensure the provision and funding of appropriately staffed, assessed and accredited training courses and inservice provision on a permanent basis, by appropriately qualified and experienced providers of adult education.

The total cost of these measures is small both absolutely and by comparison, and the expenditure would not be uneconomic. Its costs and benefits tend to fall into different departmental budgets, but there is independent evidence to show that overall savings and benefits from such a policy would exceed its total costs (Chapters 5, 8). However, society cannot reap the benefit of harnessing the initiative and the skill of volunteers unless government is prepared to trust them to know what they are about, and earns their trust.

Implications for Professions and Institutions

A variety of people serve VOs in professional capacities. They include community centre wardens, youth workers, staff working in CVSs, in community development and related projects, with self-help networks, and specialist organisations (e.g. Arts administration, Citizens' Advice Bureaux) and many others. The training currently available to them is patchy, variable, often beyond the means of those concerned and consequently under-used.

There is virtually no training for members, voluntary officers and other volunteers, except the Royal Society of Arts diploma and the internal provision of organisations such as the Keep Fit Association, the Women's Institutes, some churches and trade unions. Moreover, officials in the public services are rarely well informed about the work of voluntary organisations other than those with which they happen to have personal contact (Chapters 5, 9).

None of these gaps can be filled, nor problems solved, within current financial frameworks. In principle, what is needed is a series of integrated training patterns which can lead from volunteer induction and inservice training to professional levels via part- and full-time routes to qualification and inservice and refresher courses. To be of practical value these should involve much closer relationships between field practice and training institutions. Shared appointments, for instance, would bring the field into the institutions, would provide these with more realistic expertise and the field with more conscious and intelligent practice.

It seems likely that at some of the less specialised levels such training patterns would benefit from a degree of horizontal co-operation across different kinds of professional activity, including that of individuals employed in public services which mesh with the voluntary sector. Much of this could be developed through conferences and short courses, both for particular kinds of organisations and for cross sections of LVOs, agencies and public bodies working in a single catchment area. Such activities would certainly have implications for local CVSs and national organisations such as the National Council of Voluntary Organisations, as well as for appropriate public services at all levels. Given systematic enquiry into training needs and methods, the question of recognition would arise. This, in turn, would have implications for the Higher and Further Education Funding Councils, and training agencies.

In current conditions these matters hardly lend themselves to discussion with any degree of optimism. If change comes, planning will have to take account of then current and projected needs which cannot even be guessed at the time of writing.

Meanwhile

This project has been about adult *learning and change* in voluntary *organisations*, and its benefits to individuals, groups, communities and society at large. Its implications are wide-ranging and important. It would have been impracticable but for the very many individual men and women who helped us. What of them among all the processes, benefits, problems and crises?

We have observed people who progressed from voluntary work into training, qualification and new careers, and those whose work benefited from their membership. We found people for whom the trauma of redundancy and early retirement was mitigated by involvement and responsibility. We met those who, isolated by grief or disability, had been supported, brought into renewed health and fruitful social contact. We found those whose lives were transformed by involvement in an infinity of passionate pursuits, or by dedication to a cause, or commitment to some group or service. We witnessed people being lifted to a peak of personal fulfilment by the shared pursuit of their goal and their sense of achievement in it. Many were enabled to make useful if modest contributions to their society. And, throughout, we were aware that people were having enormous fun, and kept inventing new sources of it. However dour some pursuits might seem to the outsider, the world of voluntary organisations is a source of gaiety and joy to their members and, through them, to others. There can be few women and men in this country who escape being enlivened by them.

Conclusion

Nevertheless, the present state of the LVO sector is patchy. It remains large, active, vital and numerous. Much of it seems as yet untouched by recent social, political and economic change. Those organisations which need nothing at all from statutory sources are not directly at the mercy of government.

Our evidence demonstrates that a rich texture of VOs is *a practical advantage* to civil society. Yet financial policies which directly affect grant aid to voluntary organisations, including recent education acts, are sapping this fundamentally important part of the nation's life in four main ways. The most obvious is the reduction or removal of grant-aid, and especially of reliable core finance. The second is to price activities out of ordinary people's reach by raising fees and by depriving them of affordable accommodation in schools and colleges. The third is by introducing competitive systems which bankrupt voluntary activity by means of temporary subsidy to public institutions not making the same kind of provision. The last is the near-destruction of general adult education provided through LEA centres and their affiliation schemes for LVOs, through independent centres, the WEA, the universities, and the gross underfunding or total abandonment of major national educational voluntary organisations such as the Women's Institutes or the Educational Centres Association.

The exclusion of the great majority of the British adult population (all but the few most affluent or most deprived) from the essential educational content which forms so much of the basic framework of LVO activity, and consequently of implicit training for active citizenship, has cast a creeping blight upon the area. It is remarkable that we should have found so much in our survey that was excellent, though admittedly we made a point of looking for it. But we were conscious of much that was diminished, less effective, less well led or managed, or gone altogether. Most LVOs still embody the values of independence, of caring and co-operation, of constructive idealism, of tolerance and the search for the highest standards, and of service to the community, which we like to believe are our heritage. They remain a cornerstone of British life and society at their best and most democratic, the seedcorn of a better future. But seedcorn needs sun and rain to germinate; without them it shrivels and dies.

Yet the evidence of enthusiastic dedication, and of endurance, remains unambiguous, and some would claim to scent new hope for voluntary organisations in the air. It would be foolish to write their epitaph.

Appendices

APPENDIX 1: THE INTERVIEW AIDE-MEMOIRE

(Compressed)

A. BACKGROUND (collect separately as far as possible and supplement in interview)
1. Factual information about the catchment population, brief description of the town and its services as relevant to the survey.
2. Group programmes, activities, initiatives, membership over the years.

B. IMPACT ON MEMBERS
1. Sociable (e.g. company, friendship, something to do together with others, a new range of activities, relief from other social circumstances, etc.).
2. Educational and Cultural (e.g. learning about things or ideas, undertaking new activities, appreciating new things or activities, learning to learn, learning to co-operate, learning to discuss, to tolerate and value other opinions, learning to take responsibility, learning to organise, etc.).
3. Occupational (e.g. have any of the educational, social or personal learnings affected the ways in which members conduct their occupational activities inside/outside home? Have they affected the ways in which members are perceived by other people in these contexts? Have they affected the nature and scope of these activities, etc.?).
4. Political (e.g. has members' awareness of social/civic/political issues at any level changed? Has their level of participation changed, etc.?)
5. Personal (are members aware of any changes in themselves that would be due partly or wholly to the experience of membership, e.g. in their tastes, interests, use of time, competencies, confidence, self-knowledge?).

C. INDIRECT IMPACTS ON MEMBERS' FAMILIES / PERSONAL CONTACTS

As for B.:

1. Social
2. Educational
3. Occupational
4. Political
5. Personal

D. INDIRECT IMPACTS ON MEMBERS' OCCUPATIONAL CONTEXTS
1. In home as an occupational base ⎫
                                ⎬(using same headings as appropriate)
2. On people at work outside home ⎭
3. On the organisation / structure of work (a) at home and (b) job

E. ANY WIDER ORGANISATIONAL/CULTURAL/CIVIC/POLITICAL IMPACTS
1. as an organised group
2. as individuals

APPENDIX 2: THE ANONYMOUS QUESTIONNAIRE

(compressed)

1. Have you always lived in or near ...? Yes/No
2. If your answer was 'No', how long have you lived here? ...years
3. From where did you move to or near ....?
4. How long have you been a member of the ... group?
5. Please ring your age group:
   20–30, 31–40, 41–50, 51–60, 61–70, 71–80, 80+
   and the age at which your formal education (school, college, etc.) ended: 13   14   15   16   17   18   19   20   21   22   23   24+
6. What is your present occupation (please indicate full- or part-time), or what was your last paid employment?
7. Do you belong to any other organisations (including clubs, groups, professional, religious or political organisations) as well as the ... group? Please list all of them.
8. Have you attended any classes, courses or conferences as an adult? Yes/No
9. Please list briefly any you attended in the last 5 years and underline those which were arranged by the ... group.
10. Please list any other interests and leisure activities you have.
11. Please look again at your answers to 8, 9 and 10. Which of the organisations, activities and interests would you say grew from involvement with the ... group?
12. Please feel free to add any comments or information you think might be helpful.

APPENDIX 3: THE RETFORD POSTAL QUESTIONNAIRE

(compressed)

1. Name of Group
2. Contact person, address and telephone number
3. When was the group formed?
4. What are the group's main objectives?
5. What are the group's main activities?
6. How many members have you got at present?
   How many men?... How many women?...
   What is the age group of most members? (for instance 40–55)? ...
   How much a year does it cost to belong?...
7. Are there any paid staff? YES/NO
   How many?... and what are their roles?
8. How is the group governed or managed? (for instance "by elected officers and committee")
9. How does belonging to this group affect members? (for instance "What benefits do they gain?" "What do they learn?" "How do they change?")

   (IN THE FOLLOWING QUESTIONS 'FORMAL' MEANS REGULAR AND BY DELIBERATE ARRANGEMENT, AND 'INFORMAL' MEANS BY CHANCE, OR FROM TIME TO TIME, OR BY PERSONAL CONTACT.)

10. What formal links does your group have with any other local voluntary group? Please list these groups:
11. What informal links are there with any other local voluntary group? Please list these groups:
12. What formal links are there between your group and any agency of Local Government? (for instance social services, library, playing fields, schools etc) Please list the agencies concerned:
13. What informal links are there with any of these agencies? Please list these agencies:
14. What formal links are there between your group and professional services? (for instance doctors, solicitors, estate agents, etc.) Please list these services:
15. What informal links are there between your group and any professional services? Please list these services:
16. What formal links are there between your group and local businesses, shops, industry, trade unions? Please list those concerned:
17. What informal links are there with local business, shops, industry, unions? Please list those concerned:
18. If necessary, may we telephone you and ask for additional information to assist in the second part of this study?

    If you have a spare copy of a recent annual report we should be glad to have it, and any other additional information:

APPENDIX 4: STATISTICAL TABLES

Organisational objective	Organisations	Members	Women	Men
Sociability	8	12	14	9
Specific interest	14	21	24	16
Practical activity	30	19	5	36
Health, caring	18	9	10	8
Advocacy	13	21	20	22
Service to community	18	19	27	9

Table 1 (cp. Diagram 1): Retford: percentages of organisations by organisational objectives and percentages of members by same

TEA	Minimum	Medium	High (20+)	Totals
Strongly incongruent	53	83	51	187
Moderate/weakly incongruent	152	114	69	335
	205	197	120	522

Table 2 (cp. Diagram 7): Incongruence and TEA

Activities	1–8 activities: total	1–8 activities: w	1–8 activities: m	9–21 activities: total	9–21 activities: w	9–21 activities: m
Specialist	66	35	31	18	8	10
Generalist	35	29	6	38	31	7

Table 3 (cp. Diagram 12): Participation rates, group type and sex (N= 157)

Participation	Same: w	Same: m	Wider: w	Wider: m	Narrower: w	Narrower: m
Specialist	19	19	14	9	9	48
Generalist	6	0	50	24	2	0

Table 4 (cp. Diagram 13): History of participation, group type and sex (%) (N = 157)

TEA	Totals	Minimum	Medium	High
Women	102	16	51	35
Men	52	16	14	22

Table 5 (cp. Diagram 14): TEA and sex of respondents (N= 154)

APPENDIX 5: ARCHIVE MATERIAL, STATISTICAL PROCEDURES AND THEIR USES

Readers may recall our account of sampling procedures and the execution of our fieldwork given in Chapter 1 (pp. 4f., 6–12). To sum up, interviews were conducted in 31 case study organisations with a total of 831 individuals. This total consisted of 552 members, 68 staff and 211 observers. Anonymous questionnaires were completed by 157 individuals from 10 of the case study organisations, and details of 101 of the identified organisations at Retford were obtained by postal questionnaires, supplemented by both telephone and face to face interviews.

All the records of these operations are deposited in the archive; case studies 1 to 30 and the Retford locality study are published.

Separate data bases were constructed from the three sources. One hundred and seven variables were developed for the extremely rich source material contained in the detailed interviews with 831 individuals. They relate to the individuals concerned, the organisations, and objectives, outcomes and transmission processes. For the second data base, developed from the 157 anonymous questionnaires, the variables represented simply the questions asked. Twenty-five variables were developed for the Retford material. Analysis of the interview notes and of partial statistical results led to the categorisation of organisations into specialist and generalist, inward-looking and outward-looking, dynamic-static-divergent, etc. All three data bases were linked to this.

The Statistical Package for Social Sciences (SPSS) was used to study the data bases and, at a rough count, at least 15,000 cross-tabulations were considered. Inferences drawn from the statistical results were used only where they were significant from a chi-squared test at the 5% level. Most, however, are better than this and the great majority of those used are at the highly significant 0.1% level.

Draft text and statistics were prepared separately and then discussed and integrated. This stimulated a process of cumulative synthesis: each stage prompted further probing of the data bases, reconsideration of draft texts in the light of this, and renewed syntheses.

The data bases, the print-out material, and the statistics disk are deposited in the archive. The following table indicates the range of statistics within the main data base:

	memb	*staff*	*obser*	*spec*	*gen't*	*inwd*	*outwd*	*dyn*	*stat*	*diver*
wom.	287	45	104	125	162	222	65	150	104	33
men	265	23	107	171	94	190	75	99	121	45
totals	552	68	211	296	256	412	140	249	225	78
LVOs	31	13	31	16	15	20	11	15	10	6

APPENDIX 6: SOME GAPS IN KNOWLEDGE, AND SUGGESTIONS FOR FURTHER ENQUIRY

a.   It would be advantageous to conduct two or more further locality studies in selected areas with more substantial resources to facilitate the fullest practicable coverage. Resources permitting, one of these should investigate a larger population catchment. This would provide more and therefore more reliable knowledge of the number, distribution and characteristics of LVOs and of their members. Such studies should include occupational details, which are missing from the present study, and possibly details of LVO finances and members' time budgets.

b.   A wider study, using the matrix, should be conducted of the needs of VOs as perceived by their members, by CVS, LAs and local populations.

c.   The data bases ought to be fully exploited both for the detailed descriptive knowledge of VOs and their members which they offer, and for further research opportunities.

d.   The admitted weakness of our evidence of the mechanisms of transmission between the most immediate and the intermediate stages could be remedied by means of further intensive case studies.

e.   Detailed and intensive case studies of the processes involved in the development, transmission and effects of active citizenship are needed.

f.   Comparable studies should be conducted in selected countries to enable systematic comparative studies to be made. These could be expected to lead to useful general insights (which cannot be reliably achieved in one single society) in areas of social and community development and the study of active citizenship in civil society.

Bibliography

Allaway, A.J. (1977) *The Educational Centres Movement*, 2nd edition, Leicester: NIAE.

id. & Rawson, J. (1954) *The Rossendale Branch of the Workers' Educational Association, a brief history*, Rossendale: the Branch.

Aspinall, N. (1988) *Next to the Public Library: The story of the Percival Guildhouse, Rugby, 1925–1988*, Rugby: Percival Guildhouse.

Association of District Councils (1992) *Helping Communities Help Themselves*, London: The Association.

Aves, G.M., Committee under the chairmanship of (1969) *Report on the Voluntary Workers in the Social Services*, London: Bedford Square Press.

Barnes, B. (1986) *Learning Activity in Voluntary Organisations*, unpublished MA dissertation, University of Lancaster, being part of UDACE enquiry into Learning in Voluntary Organisations.

Batten, T.R. (1957) *Communities and their Development*, London: OUP.

id. (1965) *The Human Factor in Community Work*, London: OUP.

id. (1967) *The Non-Directive Approach in Group and Community Work*, London: OUP.

Briggs, A. & Macartney, A. (1984) *Toynbee Hall: The first hundred years*, London: RKP.

British Institute of Adult Education (1924) *The Guildhouse: A co-operative centre for adult education*, London, BIAE.

Brookfield, S. (1983) *Adult Learners, Adult Education and the Community*, Milton Keynes: the Open University Press.

Chanan, G. (1991) *Taken for Granted: Community activity and the crisis in the voluntary sector*, London: Community Development Foundation.

id. (1992) *Out of the Shadows: Strategies for local community action in Europe*, London: Community Development Foundation.

Clarke, R. (ed.) (1990) *Enterprising Neighbours*, London: NFCO and Community Projects Foundation.

Committee on Local Authority and Allied Personal Social Services (1968) *The Seebohm Report*, London: HMSO.

Darvill, G., Perkins, E. & Unell, J. (1988) *Learning from Volunteering*, Leicester: UDACE.

Duke, C. (1992) "What kind of adult education helps development?", in *Adult Education and Development*, Vol. 39, Bonn.

Education & Science, Department of (1973) *Some Aspects of the Work of the University Adult Education Centre at Nottingham*, DES.

Education, Ministry of (1944) *Community Centres* [The Red Book], London: HMSO.

Elsdon, K.T. (1962) *Centres for Adult Education*, London: NIAE.

id. (1989) "Confusion confounded, or ideas of adult education and the community", in Hake, B.J. & Morgan, W.J. (eds) *Adult Education, Public Information and Ideology*, University of Nottingham Dept of Adult Education.

id. (1991a) "Voluntary organisations, learning and democracy", in *Adult Education and Development*, Vol. 37, Bonn.

id. (1991b) *Voluntary Organisations and the White Paper*, London: Educational Centres Association.

id. (1991c) *Adult Learning in Voluntary Organisations*, Vol. 1, case studies 1 and 2, University of Nottingham Dept of Adult Education.

id. (1993) with Stewart, S. and Reynolds, J. Vol. 3, case studies 16–30 [for vols 2 and 4 see under Stewart, S. & Reynolds, J.], ib.

id. (1995) "Values and learning in voluntary organisations", in *International Journal of Lifelong Education*, Vol. 14, No. 1.

Elsey, B. (1974) "Voluntary organisations and informal adult education", in *Adult Education*, Vol. 46, No. 6, March 1974.

id. (1975) "Adult education and the 'expressive functions' of voluntary organisations", in *Vocational Aspect of Education*, Vol. XXVII, No. 68, Autumn.

id. (1993) "Voluntaryism and adult education as civil society and the 'third way' for personal empowerment and social change", *International Journal of Lifelong Education*, Vol. 12, No. 1.

Environment, Department of the (1977) *Leisure and the Quality of Life*, final report, 2 vols, London: HMSO.

Field, J. (1990) "Creating leisure", in *Adults Learning*, Vol. 2, No. 2.

Groombridge, B. (1976) "The Wincham experiment: Frank Milligan and the unemployed", in *Studies in Adult Education*, Vol. 8, No. 2.

Gulbenkian (Calouste Gulbenkian Foundation) (1968) *Community Work and Social Change*, London: Longman.

Hall, D. & Laplace, C. (1983) *Volunteers in the Adult Education Context*, Leicester: Advisory Council for Adult and Continuing Education.

Handy, C. (1988) *Understanding Voluntary Organisations*, London: Penguin.

Harris, S. & Molloy, T.N. (ND, ?1949) *The Watling Community Association: The first 21 years*, Watling CA.

Hedley, R. & Smith, J.D. (eds.) (1992) *Volunteering and Society: Principles and Practice*, London: NCVO.

Hutchinson, R. & Forrester, S. (1987) *Arts Centres in the United Kingdom*, London: Policy Studies Institute.

Jackson, K. (1973) "The marginality of community development: implications for adult education", in *International Review of Community Development*, No. 29–30, Rome.

Jennings, B. (ed.) (ND, ?1980) *Community Colleges in England and Wales*, Leicester: NIAE.

Jerman, B. (1981) *Lively-Minded Women*, London: Heinemann.

Jessup, F.W. (1951) "Post-war developments in adult education in Kent", in *Adult Education*, Vol. 24, No. 2.

Knapp, M. & Kendall, J. (1991) "Policy issues for the UK voluntary sector in the 1990s", Canterbury: University of Kent Personal Social Services Research Unit.

Knight, B. (1993) *Voluntary Action*, London: Centris/Home Office Publications.

Marks, H. (1949) *Community Centres and Adult Education*, London: National Council of Social Service.

Mee, G. & Wiltshire, H.C. (1978) *Structure and Performance in Adult Education*, London: Longman.

Nolan, C. (1992) *Leeds Widows Talking*, Leeds: National Association of Widows, Widows Advisory Service.

Percy, K. *et al.* (1983) *Post Initial Education in the North West of England: A study of provision*, Leicester: ACACE.

id. (1988) *Learning in Voluntary Organisations*, Leicester: UDACE.

Pimlott, J.A.R. (1935) *Toynbee Hall: 50 years of social progress, 1885–1934*, London: Dent.

Pre-School Playgroups Association (1981) *Parents and Playgroups*, London: Allen & Unwin.

Reynolds, J. *et al.* (1994) *A Town in Action: Voluntary networks in Retford*, being Vol. 4 of *Adult Learning in Voluntary Organisations*, Nottingham University Dept of Adult Education (for vols 1, 2, 3 see under Elsdon & Stewart).

Spencer, J. (1964) *Stress and Release in an Urban Estate*, London: Tavistock.

Stacey, M. (1960) *Tradition and Change: A study of Banbury*, OUP.

Stacey, M. *et al.* (1975) *Power, Persistence and Change: A second study of Banbury*, London: Routledge & Kegan Paul.

Stewart, S. *et al.* (1992) *Adult Learning in Voluntary Organisations*, Nottingham University Dept of Adult Education (for vols 1, 3, 4 see under Elsdon & Reynolds).

Tandon, R. (1994) "The role of voluntary action in a contemporary context: implications for institutional development", in *Adult Education and Development*, No. 42.

Tough, A. (1979) *The Adult's Learning Projects*, 2nd ed., Toronto: Ontario Institute for Studies in Education.

Trenaman, J. (1957) "Education in the adult population", in *Adult Education*, Vol. 30, No. 3; reprinted (1962) Vol. 34, No. 5, pp. 216–224.

Volunteer Centre UK, The (1991) *Voluntary Action Research Paper No. 1: Voluntary Activity – a survey of public attitudes*, London: the Centre.

Wilcox, A. (1952) "Community centres, the consumers' view", in *Adult Education*, 1952, pp. 101–111.

Wilson, A. and Ruddock, R. (1959) *After Work: leisure and learning in two towns*, London: NIAE.

Withnall, A. (1986) *The Christian Churches and Adult Education*, Leicester: NIACE.

id. (1990) "Celebrating informal learning: from theory to practice", in *Adults Learning*, Vol. 2, No. 4.

Withnall, A., Osborn, M. & Charnley, A.H. (1981) *Review of Existing Research in Adult and Continuing Education, vol. V: The Voluntary Field*, Leicester: NIACE.

Wolfenden Committee (1978) *The Future of Voluntary Organisations*, London: Croom Helm.

Index

Each of the case studies is mentioned many times in the text to illustrate research findings, but they are indexed only under their main descriptive entries. For other subjects, significant rather than exhaustive references are given.

List of Organisations Studied, with Working Titles

Case Study Organisation	Volume	Working Title
1 The 'Silverbridge' Group of the National Women's Register	1	NWR Group
2 The Ingleton (Yorks) Rural Community Association	1	Ingleton CA
3 The Percival Guildhouse, Rugby	2	Guildhouse
4 Blackfriars Arts Centre, Boston	2	Arts Centre
5 Sibsey (Lincs) Women's Institute	2	WI Group
6 Ujima (Derby)	2	Ujima
7 Stapleford and Sandiacre Rotary Club (Notts and Derbys)	2	Rotary
8 Derby Branch of the National Association of Widows	2	Widows
9 Bassetlaw Community and Voluntary Service	2	Bassetlaw CVS
10 The Macular Disease Self-Help Group	2	Macular SH
11 The Patients' Council Support Group	2	Patients' Support
12 The Arthritis Care Group	2	Arthritis SH
13 Sherwood Archaeological Society	2	Archaeologists
14 The Newstead Abbey Singers	2	Singers
15 The Midland Railway Trust	2	Railway Trust
16 The West Kirby (Wirral) Fifty-Plus Group	3	Fifty-Plus
17 The Bede House Association, Bermondsey	3	Settlement
18 A West London Community Association	3	W London CA
19 The Garibaldi and Newlands Estates Residents' Association, Mansfield	3	Residents
20 A South Wales Branch of the WEA	3	S Wales WEA
21 The Kelvedon (Essex) Branch of the WEA	3	Kelvedon WEA

22	The Sudbury Branch of the Suffolk Wildlife Trust	3	Wildlife Trust
23	The Gorgie Dalry Writers' Workshop, Edinburgh	3	Writers
24	The Long Reign Allotments Society	3	Gardeners
25	The Sutton Central (Pigeon) Flying Club	3	Pigeon Fanciers
26	The Sutton Centre Parent Teacher Association	3	PTA
27	The Holbrook (Derbys) Pre-School Playgroup	3	Playgroup
28	The Sutton Volunteer Car Scheme	3	Volunteer Drivers
29	The Aekta Carers' Self-Help Group	3	Aekta SH
30	The Llanberis Mountain Rescue Team	3	Mountain Rescue
31	An Unidentified Inner Metropolitan Welfare Organisation	not published	UIMWO
	A Town in Action (The Retford Locality Study)	*4*	*Retford*

Sampling Matrix

Key to Abbreviations

Geography	South Midland North Wales Scotland
Type of area	Rural Town City Metro Inner City
Paid staffing	None Small Medium Large
External funding	None Small Medium Large
Size of organisation	Small Medium Large
Age	1 if a major factor
Ethnicity	1 if a major factor

Matrix Entries

Main entries	bold type
Subsidiary entries	regular type

Glossary, Abbreviations and Definitions

CA   Community Association

CS   Case Study, one of the 31 carried out by the project and numbered as in flyout

CVS   Council of Voluntary Services, or Organisations

FE   Further Education

Group Size   small = 1 to 29; medium = 30 to 100; large = over 100

LA   Local Authority

LEA   Local Education Authority

LVO   Local Voluntary Organisation (see definition on p. 4)

Rate of Participation   the number of *all* sustained leisure time activities and interests in which a person is involved

Stance   one of the criteria by which organisations will be categorised. It may be "dynamic" (i.e. developing, engaged in constructive change), or "static" (i.e. unchanging, on a plateau of activity), or "divergent" (i.e. having undergone or currently undergoing changes which are negative in relation to the organisation's objectives)

TEA   Terminal Education Age, i.e. the age at which people completed their first cycle of continuous educational experience. *Minimum TEA* is defined according to what was the minimum school leaving age when particular respondents left school. Among our sample this could be 14, 15 or 16 according to their ages. *Medium TEA* is defined as any age between the minimum for that individual and 19. *High TEA* includes education to the age of 20 or above.

VO   Voluntary Organisation (generic term)

Organisation / Personal	Social service Community development Umbrellas	Advocacy	Health education Mutual support Care
Pursuit of cause	*06 Ujima MC/ISLS-1* 17 Bede House Association SMMSL-1 19 Residents' Association MTNSS--	*19 Residents' Association MTNSS--* *22 Wildlife Trust SRNNL--* 06 Ujima MC/ISLS-1 08 National Assn of Widows MCNNM1-	*29 Aekta Carers' Group MCSSS-1* 06 Ujima MC/ISLS-1 11 Patients' Support Gp MTNSS--
Give service	*02 Ingleton Community Assn NRSSL--* *09 Cmnty & Vol Service MT/RMLL--* *17 Bede House Association SMMSL-1* 11 Patients' Support Group MTNSS-- 18 West London Cmnty Assn SMMML--	*26 Parent Teacher Assn MTNNS--* 05 Sibsey Women's Institute MRNNM-- 06 Ujima MC/ISLS-1 09 Cmnty & Vol Service MT/RMLL-- 17 Bede House Association SMMSL-1 29 Aekta Carers' Group MCSSS-1	*10 Macular Disease S-H Gp MTNSS1-* *11 Patients' Support Gp MTNSS--* *12 Arthritis Care Group MTNSM1-* 17 Bede House Association SMMSL-1
Engage in sport	16 Fifty-Plus Group NTNNL1- 18 West London Cmnty Assn SMMML--		01 Silverbridge NWR MTNSS-- 16 Fifty-Plus Group NTNNL1-
Practical activity	*27 Pre-School Playgroup MRSSM--* *28 Voluntary Car Scheme MTSSS1-* 17 Bede House Association SMMSL-1 26 Parent Teacher Assn MTNNS-- 30 Mountain Rescue Team WaRNSM--	15 Midland Railway Trust MT/RLSL-- 22 Wildlife Trust SRNNL--	12 Arthritis Care Group MTNSM1- 24 Allotment Society MTNNL1- 30 Mountain Rescue Team WaRNSM--
Arts	14 Newstead Abbey Singers MT/RSNS-- 18 West London Cmnty Assn SMMML--	04 Blackfriars Arts Centre MTMSL-- 14 Newstead Abbey Singers MT/RSNS--	16 Fifty-Plus Group NTNNL1- 23 Writers' Workshop ScC/INSS--
Intellectual activity		13 Archaeological Socy MR/TNNM-- 22 Wildlife Trust SRNNL--	05 Sibsey Women's Institute MRNNM-- 03 P Guildhouse Rugby MTSSL1- 20 A South Wales WEA Gp WaRNSM1- 21 Kelvedon Br WEA SRNNM-- 23 Writers' Workshop ScC/INSS--
Social contact	07 Rotary Club MTNNS1- 17 Bede House Association SMMSL-1 18 West London Cmnty Assn SMMML-- 28 Voluntary Car Scheme MTSSS1-	09 Cmnty & Vol Service MT/RMLL-- 17 Bede House Association SMMSL-1	10 Macular Disease S-' ' Gp MTNSS1- 11 Patients' Support Gp MTNSS-- 12 Arthritis Care Group MTNSM1- 28 Voluntary Car Scheme MTSSS1- 29 Aekta Carers' Group MCSSS-1

Characteristics of LVOS

Physical activity	Specific interests Hobbies	Sociability	Provision for women
	19 Residents' Association MTNSS-- 22 Wildlife Trust SRNNL--	08 National Assn of Widows MCNNM1- 10 Macular Disease S-H Gp MTNSS1- 11 Patients' Support Gp MTNSS-- 12 Arthritis Care Group MTNSM1-	05 Sibsey Women's Institute MRNNM-- 08 National Assn of Widows MCNNM1- 27 Pre-School Playgroup MRSSM--
30 Mountain Rescue Team WaRNSM--	02 Ingleton Community Assn NRSSL-- 24 Allotment Society MTNNL1-	02 Ingleton Community Assn NRSSL-- 05 Sibsey Women's Institute MRNNM-- 07 Rotary Club MTNNS1- 26 Parent Teacher Assn MTNNS--	*08 National Assn of Widows MCNNM1-* 05 Sibsey Women's Institute MRNNM-- 27 Pre-School Playgroup MRSSM--
16 Fifty-Plus Group NTNNL1- 02 Ingleton Community Assn NRSSL-- 18 West London Cmnty Assn SMMML-- 30 Mountain Rescue Team WaRNSM--	02 Ingleton Community Assn NRSSL-- 18 West London Cmnty Assn SMMML-	*18 West London Cmnty Assn SMMML--* 01 Silverbridge NWR MTNNS-- 05 Sibsey Women's Institute MRNNM-- 10 Fifty-Plus Group NTNNL1-	16 Fifty-Plus Group NTNNL1-
30 Mountain Rescue Team WaRNSM-- 24 Allotment Society MTNNL1-	*15 Midland Railway Trust MT/RLSL--* *24 Allotment Society MTNNL1-* *25 Pigeon Club MTSNM1-* 13 Archaeological Socy MR/TNNM-- 27 Pre-School Playgroup MRSSM--	15 Midland Railway Trust MT/RLSL-- 22 Wildlife Trust SRNNL-- 24 Allotment Society MTNNL1-	05 Sibsey Women's Institute MRNNM-- 17 Bede House Association SMMSL-1
18 West London Cmnty Assn SMMML--	*04 Blackfriars Arts Centre MTMSL--* *14 Newstead Abbey Singers MT/RSNS--* *23 Writers' Workshop ScC/INSS--*	01 Silverbridge NWR MTNNS-- 02 Ingleton Community Assn NRSSL-- 04 Blackfriars Arts Centre MTMSL-- 14 Newstead Abbey Singers MT/RSNS-- 16 Fifty-Plus Group NTNNL1-	05 Sibsey Women's Institute MRNNM--
15 Midland Railway Trust MT/RLSL-- 22 Wildlife Trust SRNNL-- 24 Allotment Society MTNNL1- 13 Archaeological Socy MR/TNNM--	*03 P Guildhouse Rugby MTSSL1-* *13 Archaeological Socy MR/TNNM--* *20 A South Wales WEA Gp WaRNSM1-* *21 Kelvedon Br WEA SRNNM--* 23 Writers' Workshop ScC/INSS-- 22 Wildlife Trust SRNNL-- 25 Pigeon Club MTSNM1-	13 Archaeological Socy MR/TNNM-- 20 A South Wales WEA Gp WaRNSM1- 21 Kelvedon Br WEA SRNNM--	*01 Silverbridge NWR MTNNS--* *05 Sibsey Women's Institute MRNNM--*
02 Ingleton Community Assn NRSSL-- 16 Fifty-Plus Group NTNNL1-	03 P Guildhouse Rugby MTSSL1- 16 Fifty-Plus Group NTNNL1- 23 Writers' Workshop ScC/INSS-- 24 Allotment Society MTNNL1-	*07 Rotary Club MTNNS1-*	01 Silverbridge NWR MTNNS-- 05 Sibsey Women's Institute MRNNM--